JOURNAL
of a
WALLEYE PRO

To Patrick –
Good fishing
Daryl Christensen

DARYL CHRISTENSEN
WITH BERNIE BARRINGER

Journal of a Walleye Pro

Daryl Christensen as told to Bernie Barringer

Published and Printed in the USA.

First Printing, February, 1999

ISBN# 1-885149-08-5

Electronic prepress by
Moving Mountain Publishing
P.O. Box 40
Crsytal Lake, IA 50432
(515) 565-3389
Exceptional outdoor books and magazines

Photos by Bernie Barringer, Sherry Christensen or Daryl Christensen

Front cover photoof Daryl by Jim Kalkofen,
Background cover photos by Juris Ozols
Back cover photo of Daryl by Jim Kalkofen
Back cover photo of Bernie by Steve Weisman

Cover design by Juris Ozols

Daryl's Acknowledgments

It doesn't take many people to make a book, but it takes a whole bunch to make a career. Many of them have become lifelong friends. If I've forgotten anyone, please forgive me.

First of all, I want to thank Bernie Barringer for giving me the idea for this book. Without him, it wouldn't have been written. Thanks to my wife Sherry, for her understanding, and my kids who could have benefited by me being home more often.

Sponsorship is the lifeblood of professional fishing. Without them, there would be no tournament circuit or pro anglers. The list is long, but all are much appreciated. Mercury Marine, my first sponsor. Thanks to Jim Kalkofen who helped me from the beginning while he was at Mercury and later at the PWT. He's become a great friend. Dan Schaad, Mike Phillips, Dave Bytner and Pam Behnke all from Mercury.

Fisher and Starcraft Boats: from the early years; John Reese, Harold Stalter, Steve Mason and all the Mercury Powerboats Team. Brunswick Marine: John Charvat and Jim Dawson. Fisher Boats today: Mike Fine, Gary Rusk, Dave Simmons and Steve Mason.

The fine folks at Zebco/Quantum/MotorGuide: Gary Dollihon, Lance Peck, Jim Dawson and Ginger. From Wille Products: Jean Schick. Bait Rigs Tackle: Joe and Tony Puccio. Mann's Baits: Frank Delrich, Lanny Deal and Suzanne Newsome. Stren Fishing Lines: Mark Fisher and Jennifer Haldus. Mustad Hooks: Chuck Reynolds and Skip. From Red-D-Light: Dan Toy, Rich Graves and Bruce Cayce. Ocean Waves Sunglasses: Gary Moran and Chris Beeksma.

Past sponsors from the MWC days helped launch my career with their support: Doelcher Products; Pradco; Lindy-Little Joe; Zercom Marine; Berkley; Hobie Sunglasses; Federal Telecom; Dodge Trucks; Good Old Day's Resort; D-Scent; Blitz Lures; Jig-A-Whopper and B & M Boatseats.

Television can get a pro's face and name out there quicker than anything and I want to thank the following TV people for putting me on their shows: The folks at ESPN and TNN; In-Fisherman (Mike Simpson, you're the best in the business!); Babe Winkelman; John Gillespie; Dan Small; my late friend, Dick Rose; and the great numbers of regional and local television crews.

Outdoor writers and photographers get an angler's face and facts before the public daily. There are so many that I've worked with over the years. Again, I apologize if I've forgotten anyone. Dave Mull, outdoor writer and my MWC partner in 1990 and his wife, Kathy. Dave Csanda; Matt Straw; Steve Quinn and Jan Couch, all from In-Fisherman. Freelancers and outdoor writers: Larry Porter, Mark Strand, Mark Romanack, Monte Burch, Jim Spencer, Terry Wickstrom, Jim Churchill, Doug Stamm, Terry Koper, Ron Leys, Bob Kaczkowski; Clayton Dyskrud; Jeff Murray and a host of others.

You can't be successful without mentors and friends to help you along the way. In the fishing business I want to acknowledge Mike McClelland for his guidance. Gary Parsons and Keith Kavajecs for their early support and continued level of competition! Ron and Delores Lindner for their support and friendship; Al and Mary Lindner for the same. Mark Dorn for his spiritual guidance; Craig Reiger for his hard work in locating sponsors; Jeff Shannon, Scott Hauge, Roger Smith, Gary Gray, Kim Papineau, Bill Klotzbucher and Dick Stille for sharing their fishing, knowledge. And all of the friends I've made on the tournament trail over the years. I especially want to thank Scott Hill who taught me a lot about tournament fishing and really lit the fire under me to go out and compete on a national level. He's still one of the best walleye fishermen I've ever known. Thanks also to Ken Gentry, my MWC partner in 1989. His support was the catalyst into the Professional Walleye Trail. Thanks, Ken, I couldn't have done it without you.

Finally, and most importantly, I want to thank Pastor Sam Timm and all the folks at Wautoma Assembly of God as well as my many friends around the country who pray for me at each tournament. Those prayers are a great encouragement to me and my family. Thank you, Lord, for answering those prayers, and being with me daily the past 10 years on the tournament trail.

Bernie's Acknowledgements

I would like to thank Daryl for putting so much of his time and effort into this book. I would like to thank the fine folks, primarily Mark Dorn and Jim Kalkofen, at In-Fisherman Professional Walleye Trail for their cooperation and help in getting me what I needed to make this project a success. Special gratitude to Ron and Al Lindner, who—since I first came across In-Fisherman magazine back in 1978—have in so many ways influenced my angling and my life.

Most of all, I would like to thank my lovely and patient wife of 20 years, Cheri, who has put up with so much in order to allow me to chase my dream of making a living in the outdoors. Through fat times and more often lean, never once has she told me to get a real job.

Contents

Introduction

Speeding down Lake Ouachita, Daryl's eyes, moving continuously, scanned the shoreline, the islands, the weeds and the flooded timber; anything that might give him a clue about the lake's walleyes. It was the first day of prefishing for the Walleye Super Pro, an event to which only the top walleye anglers are invited. The top 40 all-time money winners on the Professional Walleye Trail (PWT) come to this event to compete for $180,000 in cash and prizes. The stakes are high, the rewards to the winner are immeasurable in the long-term benefits to a professional angler. This intensity was reflected in Daryl's conversation, his attitude, I could see it even in his demeanor.

Suddenly, Daryl cranked the boat to the left, heading directly toward a flock of birds floating on the calm surface. The thought occurred to me that not many of the contestants looked to birds for clues to the location of walleyes. At least not on southern reservoirs in the early spring. When the boat dropped off plane, Daryl reached into a compartment and pulled out a binoculars. "Could be Bonaparte's gulls," he said, looking through the glass. He then opened another compartment and produced a field guide to bird identification. Soon he found the page he was looking for. "Yup, Bonapate's gulls. Surprised to see them so far south this time of the year." He then tossed the book and binoculars back in the compartment, wheeled the boat around and headed on down the lake. "I'm a serious birder," he said, "I even guide birders back in Wisconsin when I'm not fishing." His interest in those gulls had nothing to do with walleyes at all!

This Daryl Christensen is a complex individual.

Daryl also pursues fur trapping and many types of hunting. If it's done outdoors, he's probably done it. Even during the intensity of fishing in a PWT tournament, I've seen Daryl look to the trees and identify a bird by its call. I've seen him take his eyes off his line for a moment, visually take in the natural beauty of a steep rocky bluff, take a deep breath, then go back to fishing.

I don't know any tournament fishermen who do it for the money. There are a lot of things you could do that are a lot less stressful, a lot less work, at which you could make more money. One thing is for sure, Daryl Christensen is a professional fisherman primarily because he loves fishing and all the things that go with it.

When I came up with the idea to do this book, I did not know Daryl. As an outdoor writer, I'd had the pleasure of fishing with many professional anglers. When I set out do do this book, I knew what I needed. I needed an angler I could trust. One who would not steal the idea, one who would not put something in the book to take a cheap shot at a competitor. An angler who was respected by his peers for not only his angling skill but his integrity. One whose name would be recognized among the anglers who would be potential buyers of the book. And one who should finish well on the scheduled waters.

It took a fair amount of research, but when I introduced myself to Daryl on the phone that February day, I already knew that he was my man, if he would agree to do it. Fortunately, he did. And I'm proud to say that he is perfect for this task. I think you will agree by the time you come to the end of the book.

Daryl and I discussed what we thought anglers would want out of a book like this. Then I gave Daryl his assignment. It was easy to say, but very difficult to do. Tape record your actions, thoughts and ideas. That's it. Tell the readers how you feel after a long stint of physically and emotionally draining sports show appearances. Tell them about the headaches of working with sponsors. Tell them how you feel after a great day on the water. Tell them what it's like to stand up on stage and accept a big check—for catching fish! What is it *really* like to be a professional angler? Tell them.

Well, tell you is exactly what he has done! He really opened his heart and soul in this book, holding nothing back. You'll learn a lot about fishing as a professional here, and you get to know Daryl Christensen like few people know him. Daryl really opens his heart to you late in the book when he discussees his regrets about lost time that could have been with his family. He also goes into a fairly lengthy discussion of his spiritual beliefs and how they affect his life. Some might say such things have no place in a book like this. To really understand Daryl, you must understand his world view and how his beliefs affect every decision he makes. To leave that out would be to leave out who Daryl really is. I decided to leave it exactly as he tells it.

On these pages, you will see into the world of professional walleye angling like you've never seen it before. I hope you enjoy reading it as much as we enjoyed bringing it to you.

Bernie Barringer

Foreword

Walleye fishing is booming! Today there is greater awareness of walleye fishing and increasing popularity in the sport than ever before. And for good reasons. Thanks to the regulation of walleye waters and the management of fish populations by the Departments of Natural Resources and the U.S. Department of Fish and Wildlife Service, walleye anglers are experiencing the best walleye fishing in years.

What's more, the sport of walleye fishing has grown tremendously over the past 10 years with the creation of the In-Fisherman Professional Walleye Trail (PWT) tournament circuit. Now for the first time walleye fishing receives exposure in magazines and on national television and radio, attracting top sponsors along with the best walleye anglers in the world. And that's where Daryl Christensen enters the fishing scene.

Living close to some of the best walleye waters in Wisconsin, Lake Winnebago, Daryl fine tuned his walleye fishing skills and was known locally as a "hot stick." He was successful fishing the local walleye and bass tournaments and soon realized he could make a living from fishing. You'll discover many of Daryl's secret strategies and benefit from his many years of "on-the-water" experience when reading about his prefishing strategies and his tactics for finding winning fish. You'll get some valuable insights into the sponsorship side of professional angling, and you'll look deep into the personal life and thoughts of one of the premiere professional anglers of our day.

Daryl is not only a good fisherman, but a skilled communicator who represents the sport and his sponsors with integrity. He is a loyal ambassador to the sport of walleye fishing and is my idea of what a true role model should be.

I'm proud to be his friend.

Al Lindner

Preseason 1997

Journal of a Walleye Pro

It isn't often that a person can have a dream come true 20 years after the initial dream. It happened to me, though, and I've always thought that my story would be one that would be of interest to others. After all, the most-asked question on the speaking tour is "How do I become a fishing pro?" or "What's it like being a pro fisherman?"

So when author and outdoor writer, Bernie Barringer asked if I would be interested in teaming up with him to write a book about my life on the professional walleye circuit, I responded with a hearty "YES!"

While this book doesn't necessarily tell about my whole life on the tournament trail, it does expose the many ups and downs of tournament life, as well as some of the unique events on the In-Fisherman Professional Walleye Trail and other tournaments.

Our goal in writing this book was to bring the reader along on the road and on the water to experience, first hand, what professional tournament fishing is all about. So come along and feel the wind in your face, the hot sun beating down on your neck, the disappointments and victories, the day-by-day and month-by-month events that shape the Professional Walleye Trail.

February 10, 1997

"How do you want to go about doing this?" I asked Bernie Barringer at our first meeting in Dubuque, Iowa on February 10th, 1997. It seemed fitting to me that our meeting would be at Dave Lincoln's Bait Shack on the frozen Mississippi River. Crossing the Highway 151 bridge en-route to the meeting, I couldn't help but reminisce on winning my first major walleye tournament almost 10 years ago only a few miles downstream from the bridge.

I related that story and many others to Bernie as we got to know one another on a more personal basis, building a bridge of our own, of sorts, into a relationship that would eventually lead to the development of this book. It was his idea, and a good one, that I should record my daily activities on the tournament trail, as well as promotional trail, like sort of a diary, and that I should begin this journal today.

So *Journal of a Walleye Pro* starts on February 10th, 1997 and continues through two seasons on the walleye tournament trail and sportshow circuit, ending with the close of the season in 1998. A lot of water has passed under the Hwy 151 bridge since we first got together with this idea, just like a lot of time has passed in both our lives.

As I'm driving back home after our meeting, I write half of the book in my mind, months before the season even starts. I'm sure that's why Bernie wanted the journal, so that people reading this could share, not only in the seasonal experiences, but in the daily ones as well.

Wednesday February 19th

I'm in Beloit, Wisconsin, about two hours from home, and just finished speaking to the Rock Valley Anglers, a club well-known to guys on the speakers circuit. In fact, I first spoke at this club about 15 years ago and found them to be as interested and friendly today as they were back then. As is the case with most seminars, I could have stayed and talked all night about fishing, but I drove home after the event, as I often do if I'm within a few hours of home. Being on the road a lot, it's always nice to take every advantage I can to sleep in my own bed.

Thursday, February 20th

I'm in Green Bay, Wisconsin giving a seminar on river walleyes, and I must say that there couldn't be a more exciting time to be in this city, following the Packer's recent Super Bowl victory. But the folks here tonight are much more interested in catching big walleyes from the Fox River, which flows right through the middle of Titletown.

River walleyes have always been my favorites, having been born and raised upstream from Green Bay on the Fox River itself. It was a great night of sharing memories of fishing the Fox both in my backyard and spots between there and Green Bay. The pay wasn't bad either!

Friday and Saturday, February 21-22

I left Green Bay in a snowstorm (does it always snow in Green Bay?) after the seminar, since I had to be at the Madison Fishing Expo in Madison, Wisconsin the next two days. I love the Expo and was the keynote speaker at their first event 10 years ago. The Expo donates most of their proceeds to lake improvement projects in the Madison area, so it's always a privilege to be a part of their event.

Al Lindner was the speaker this weekend and in between seminars, we had a great opportunity to get caught up on each other's schedules as well as our families. I told him about the book I was working on and he agreed to help in any way. That's Al: as down-to-earth as ever and a great mentor and friend. As always he was true to his word as he agreed to do the Foreword for this book.

As is the case with most seminars, I could have stayed and talked all night about fishing, but I drove home after the event, as I often do if I'm within a few hours of home. Being on the road a lot, it's always nice to take every advantage I can to sleep in my own bed.

Sunday, February 23rd

After morning church with my wife, Sherry, I blasted over to Mauston, Wisconsin to spend the afternoon with a Fisher dealer at their annual sport and fishing show. It was tough staying awake on the way home, as the long days and nights of the past week were taking their toll. Fortunately, I have Monday free before driving to Springfield, Missouri for the Bass Pro Shops Spring Classic.

Tuesday, February 25th

It's early Tuesday morning and Sherry and I are driving south to Springfield. It's a 12-hour trip from home, but I'm looking forward to speaking at the Spring Classic. It's going to be fun to compete in the "fish-off" tournament against the bass guys and other walleye pros. I'm also scheduled to speak at several seminars and work the Mann's, Quantum, and Stren booths.

Wednesday, February 26th

Although the Spring Classic doesn't officially start until tomorrow, the shoppers know that several fishing pros will be around, so the Bass Pro Shops store is already a zoo. I spent most of the day browsing around, talking to manufacturer's reps, renewing old acquaintances and talking fishing with shoppers and local anglers. It's one of those days where you "do lunch" about six times as you run into various friends and sponsors. If I keep this lunching up, I'm going to have to order a bigger boat!

Thursday, February 27th

Seminar time, and the place is packed. I did a walleye forum with Sam Anderson, Ross Grothe, Perry Good and Doc Johnson. It was fun doing a forum with these young guys. I learned some interesting stuff from listening to their theories on fishing, and their reliance on electronics and GPS technology. These guys are hot sticks and great representatives of their sport. It was a pleasure sharing the stage with them, although it would be great fun to fish against them without any electronics or navigation. (Am I really getting that old?)

Friday, February 28th

I'm on my way to Nixa, Missouri on Highway 65 South, going down to pick up this year's boat, a Fisher Hawk 181 dual console. I'm getting all geared up for the tournament fishing season and I'm pretty excited. After spending the past two days at Bass Pro doing walleye seminars, I can see that there is great interest in the walleye tournament trail even way down here in the South.

The first tournament will be the Walleye Super Pro on Lake Ouachita in Arkansas, not too far from Springfield. I've already gotten a lot of good information from people who stopped by the booth and told me about where and how they fish down there. I'm getting pretty pumped up about it!

I've had a lot of good meetings this week, visiting with some of the bass and walleye pros, just talking shop, talking business, like we all need to do. After all, you have to treat this like a business to do it right. The Bass Pro Shops Spring Classic is kind of the kickoff to our tournament season. The bass guys are already fishing because there isn't any ice on these lakes down here. There's plenty of it back home, however, so it's really nice to come down here. As I walk through the store, I get charged up—talking with sponsors, talking with the industry people. They're very upbeat, very positive about the future. Even though the fishing industry is on a downturn at this time, they're optimistic as always and that's a good thing. I think it's going to get better soon. I think we're going to see an upturn again as we always have. I'm starting to get in the tournament mind-set from visiting with the tournament guys and just getting fired up.

The trip to pick up the boat went without a hitch, literally. (I managed to find one in my box of spare parts in the back of the suburban). Actually, I really did have a hitch on the truck, but needed a raised hitch for the new trailer. Fortunately, I had one along. I got back to Bass Pro just in time for my Friday seminar and to do very badly in the "fish off". Electronic bass just don't fight the same as the real ones. The bass guys won the event, but some were given second chances for one reason or another. Kind of reminded me of Tanya Harding at the Olympics. (Just kidding, of course).

Saturday, March 1st

March has finally arrived. I've been waiting for this day for... well, since October. March means the lakes and rivers are going to be opening up and I can start doing some fishing. I'm walking across the parking lot at Bass Pro and a nice little rain shower is falling. There's something about the fragrance of spring rain on blacktop that gets the walleye fishing blood boiling. It's kind of like that first snowfall for deer season, or first cold front in fall that sends hordes of ducks spiraling downward from the north across the waterfowlers bobbing decoys.

I'm grateful for the shower and happy to finish the day of speaking. I'll be driving most of the night, towing my new boat home. I might even get a chance to do some fishing when I get there, since the weather forecast looks good for central Wisconsin. As I'm driving northeast on Highway 44, I can't help but think how well the show went. There's a lot of interest in walleye fishing—major interest in walleye fishing down here in the mid-south. I think that we're going to see a real surge of excitement regarding this type of fishing down here. It will be supplemental to bass fishing of course. It obviously will never overtake bass in this part of the country, but it'll be a good diversion from casting spinnerbaits, flippin' pigs and jigs and Carolina Riggin'. This year I saw the most interest ever since we've been coming down here the last four years. In speaking to the good folks down here about walleye fishing, I get a good feel for what their interests are.

Driving long distances provides many hours of thinking time. I recalled the years of when I would get the Bass Pro Shops catalog and see the pictures of all the pros in it and the lures they were promoting. I remembered my dream of being like one of those guys someday. Now I'm driving back from the show, having been a speaker and promoter and having my photo in the catalog just like them. It was surreal. Was this real or was I still dreaming? My photo in the same catalog with Al Lindner, Roland Martin, Jimmy Houston, Gary Roach, Bill Dance and all the other famous professional fishermen? People who years ago were my heroes, who I now call associates and even friends?

I remember being in awe of Roland, Al and Bill Dance at the Chicago Sportshow back in the early 80's; too shy to even approach them for an autograph, or even dare to imagine fishing with them someday. Today, they are friends with whom I have fished, eaten lunch, and spent endless hours talking business, and there are many others.

As long as I live, I'll always remember my first Masters Walleye Circuit tournament on the Illinois River. Getting ready for the take-off, I looked to my left and saw Gary Roach and Randy Amenrud. To my right was Bob Propst and Mike McClelland. I was in awe. Today they are all friends and peers. Yes, the dream had indeed become a reality.

Monday, March 3rd

The trip from Springfield was uneventful, save for a lot of weird thoughts that come from being tired and staring at 600 miles of road illuminated 100 yards at a stretch by headlights. It's almost like driving through a 600-mile tunnel with blackness on both sides and the only light in front. It can make a person goofy. I prefer to use the term "buzzy". Lack of sleep and too much caffeine makes every cell vibrate. Yes, "buzzy" is the right word.

As I drive across the bridge on Highway 22 in Montello, I look over at the dam below Buffalo Lake to see if the ice is breaking up. I caught my first walleye ever in the south corner of the dam. I have remembered it the thousands of times I've passed that bridge since. One year the walleyes came up the river on March 6th, and I'm thinking about that as I looked at the ice-covered lake. "Not this year," I muse. Besides, I don't really have time to fish. I have to get my new boat home, get it rigged and pick up last year's boat at Norton's Dry Dock in Green Lake where it's getting prepped for sale to a friend from Bismarck, North Dakota.

An early spring is trying to happen here in south-central Wisconsin. There's still a lot of snow, but some bare ground and a few red-winged blackbirds and robins along with a warm, south wind are getting me fired up to get the boat rigged and get out fishing. But it's going to be a busy week.

Dave Norton, owner of Norton's Dry Dock, greeted me with "you look like you've been on a three-day drunk", to which I replied I had driven all night and needed to pick up the boat to take to Minnetonka, Minnesota in the morning.

"Same thing," he replied.

I picked up the boat and headed home. Upon checking my schedule, I discovered that I didn't have to take the boat to Minnetonka tomorrow, but on Wednesday. I actually have a meeting with Bait Rigs Tackle in Madison on Tuesday. I need to get back from Minnetonka right away because Thursday I'll be speaking to the workers at Mercury Marine and thanking them for the good job they've done this year and just the good job they've done in quality craftsmanship on the engines that I run. I want to show them my appreciation for keeping me up and running on the water at all the tournaments and other promotional times. Friday I'll be heading down to Chicago where Saturday I'll be speaking at the Walleye Institute. So it's going to be a busy week. My son, Sean, is coming back from college for spring break. He'll be introducing us to his new girlfriend, Heather. We're hoping to get out and do some fishing—some catchin'-up time together. It's that time of the year—we're really gearing up and going full bore in the promotional end and it won't be long and it'll be April and that's fishin' time.

Thursday, March 6th

My schedule finally caught up with me on Tuesday night and I decided not to go to Minnesota with the boat until later next week, since I have to be in Minneapolis anyway for a seminar. Instead, I rested up yesterday and am now on my way to Fond du Lac, Wisconsin to speak to the workers at Mercury Marine. I'm really looking forward to this day—to share some fishing secrets with them, but also shake hands throughout the factory and thank the workers for the good job they've done in their work, craftsmanship and dedication to putting out a product that keeps me on the water. You know, in 10 years of full-time tournament fishing, I've never had an engine break down during a tournament. That's a rarity in any industry, and I'm really appreciative to these people for putting out such a quality product. These engines not only have gotten me to the fish in every tournament, they've also gotten me back to weigh them in at the end of the day.

As I'm heading east toward Fond du Lac this morning, I see snow banks piled up all over the place. Boy, it looks like spring is never going to come, but I know it won't be long and I'll be out on the water. I'm really getting more than anxious to do it and, well, even with all the snow, I know that it only takes a few warm days to knock it down. It's still sport show and seminar time and I guess if the weather was nice I'd wish I wasn't doing seminars and I was out fishing somewhere. So actually, the bad weather isn't all that bad, since I have to be inside doing seminars anyway. I really am looking forward to today and I'm also looking forward to spring coming soon.

Friday, March 7th

I'm heading south and east, just entering Illinois, heading for Chicago to do the Walleye Institute with my friend and fellow competitor, Ted Takasaki. The Mercury event went well, but I didn't get home until 10:30 last night. Following the seminar, I had several meetings, a plant tour and dinner. It went really well, and I hope to do it again real soon.

I'm excited about doing a Walleye Institute, although I find it somewhat ironic that a guy who used to skip school to go fishing, now is skipping a day of fishing to teach school. Sometimes life gets pretty weird, if you know what I mean. The traffic is jammed up pretty tight coming into Chicago and I'm really looking forward to getting out of this truck and into the Holiday Inn for some R & R before starting a day of classes tomorrow.

Saturday, March 8

The Institute was a huge success and fun to do. Ted Takasaki gives an awesome seminar and it was a privelege to work with him. Sean and Heather met us at the Holiday Inn after a long drive from South Carolina. We had a great time of catching up on the way home and planning for the week ahead which would include three seminars in three different cities.

Monday, March 10

Back to Green Bay for another seminar, this time with Sean and

Appearances before even small crowds at open houses, boat dealers and fishing clubs are an important part of keeping sponsors happy.

Heather along. We toured Lambeau Field and the Packer Hall of Fame. Even Heather, a Miami Dolphins fan, was impressed. Of course the moment we arrived in Green Bay it started to snow (big surprise), much to the delight of the two transplanted Southerners and chagrin of the driver, being me. The seminar was hugely attended and went very well. Even my son, Steve, and his friends attended, driving up from Oshkosh. During my talk, my throat started getting sore and I knew what was coming down the road.

If there's one thing I really hate, it's getting sick during the sportshow season. It seems inevitable, however, with all the hands you shake and all the people you come in contact with. It happens every February or March for me, put I just have to power through it. The way I feel right now, I don't know how I'm going to be able to speak anywhere this week.

Thursday, March 13th

We're being greeted this morning by the biggest blizzard of the year and I'm supposed to be at Norton's Dry Dock tonight to do a seminar on advanced angling techniques. This is an annual event at the Marina this time of year, but it's likely it will be canceled. That's okay because I can barely talk and feel really lousy. Sean and Heather are planning on driving back to South Carolina today. Not a great idea. It's early evening and over a foot of snow has fallen since morning. Norton's decided to have the seminar anyway, so off I go. As I'm driving to Green Lake in the swirling snow, all I can think of is W.C. Fields' famous line: "It's not a fit night out for man nor beast." I laugh. Who would be crazy enough to come to a fishing seminar on a night like this. I'm greeted by 55 fishermen, hungry to learn advanced angling techniques.

At 10:00 p.m. I climb back into the suburban totally hoarse and burning with fever. I have a day to rest up before driving to Minneapolis on Saturday. I want to call and cancel, but just can't bring myself to do it after all the publicity for the seminar with Gary Roach at Galyon's. It's snowing so hard on the way home, that I can barely see the road. The 20 mile trip takes 40 minutes. Prior to the storm, the snow had all melted, it looked like spring was coming. Robins, blackbirds and sandhill cranes were everywhere, and the winter wheat was greening up. I feel sorry for these early spring birds. The rivers were opening, too, and walleyes were moving, starting to stage in places. But right now, it's gotten awful ugly out there.

Saturday morning, March 15th

It continued to snow all day Friday, postponing Sean and Heather's trip to South Carolina. As they rejoiced and played in the snow, I wished I WAS in South Carolina. My plan was to drive to Burnsville, Minnesota this morning and drop off last year's boat to the guy who bought it. Then I was to head on over to Galyon's and do a seminar with Gary Roach, and an in-store promotion for Quantum/MotorGuide. But I'm looking at 16 inches of fresh snow on the ground and 30 inches just 10 miles north of here. I'm still going to head out, but decided to leave the boat because of the bad road conditions. I'll drive up without it, and probably have to turn around and make the trip again in a couple of days. It's only about 250 miles one way, so I can handle that later next week. I just can't believe how much the snow has piled up and the air temperature is two below zero. On the 15th of March we should be having spring, but it doesn't look like spring is going to happen for awhile. The good news is that I'll be heading down to the first tournament in Arkansas in 25 days, and right now, that's something I'm really looking forward to.

I find it somewhat ironic that a guy who used to skip school to go fishing is now skipping a day of fishing to teach school. Sometimes life gets pretty weird, if you know what I mean.

The Galyon's seminars went really well, and it was really great working with my old friend, Mr. Walleye, Gary Roach. We had a super time sharing stories with the customers and just talking tournament fishing. Both of us are getting geared up for the year and it was just good to see old Roach again. The in-store went real well and I sold some rods and Energy reels for Quantum. It's late afternoon and I'm heading south on I-94 back home. I've got a meeting tonight at 8:00 and I should just about make it.

Monday night, March 17th St. Patrick's Day

I spoke at the Christian Women's Club Men's Night in Waupaca, Wisconsin and it was a very good night. We had 68 people listen to a seminar on fishing the Professional Walleye Trail and I shared my personal testimony of how God had changed my life. Ten people made a decision for Christ that night. It was a great night. I've been fighting a nasty cold all week, it has been tough just getting up in the morning. But that makes it all worth it.

Wednesday, March 19th

One day of rest, but I'm still feeling lousy, as I drive north on I-94 back to Minnetonka with last year's boat in tow. I drop the boat off at the buyer's brother's house, and his wife gives me the check. Will I ever get rid of this cold? I see the Mississippi River is wide open and people are fishing below the dams. Walleyes are biting and I wish I could join them, but I have a seminar tomorrow night and Friday night and Saturday in Milwaukee and my boat's not rigged yet. Next week I'll sit down and get my boat ready, then maybe take a couple of trips down it on the Wisconsin River and catch some walleyes in my old stompin' grounds. I need to get the boat broken in and get my new rods and reels broken in and see how they feel. It's getting close. It's getting to be time to get with it.

Friday, March 21st

I'm on my way to the Milwaukee Sentinel Sport & Travel Show where I'll be doing a seminar this evening on spring walleye tactics. Last night, I spoke at the Odd Fellows meeting in Portage, Wisconsin. I discussed several tactics for walleye fishing, as well as how to become a professional angler. I also opened it up for questions and the service club members had several, mostly on conservation issues. It was an enjoyable evening.

Today I'll have another opportunity to do a questions and answer period as well as continue to promote the book. I'm looking forward to being in Milwaukee and seeing some old friends. It's the last major show of the year before I head down to Arkansas. I'll have a few other seminars in between the tournaments this summer, but primarily, this is the last big show. I'm kind of anxious to get the show season over and head south.

Sunday, March 23rd

Milwaukee went really well. I am kind of sad but also relieved that the show season is finally over, even though I do enjoy sharing fishing information with people. The crowds were great in Milwaukee, with the attendance up 34% over last year. People attending the seminars asked good questions and they were a very polite audience. It was interesting that, once again, conservation issues were raised. I like addressing these types of questions, because I think it shows the general public that many of us pro fishermen are as concerned as they are about water quality issues, overharvest, stocking programs, etc. While I was at the show, I noticed water running all over the street outside. The warm, spring weather was returning and I was more fired up than ever to get out fishing.

Wednesday, March 26th
It's an unbelievable day. The high hit 73 degrees and the snow and ice are melting like crazy! I peeled the shrink wrap off my boat today and started rigging it up. It only took me about four hours to put in the batteries, locators, marine radio and rod holders. She's just about ready to go. I still need to install an auxiliary gas tank for my 9.9 kicker (it also serves as emergency gas to get back if the water gets rough), and get a new compass, flare gun kit and distress flag before I can fish the first tournament. Every year when I load this stuff in the boat, I feel like I'm outfitting a Coast Guard vessel instead of a fishing boat. But it is a good feeling to know all this

No taking it easy in the off-season. A continual string of sportshow seminars makes the winter fly.

stuff is on board when you head out in six-footers on Lake Erie or Saginaw Bay.

Only a few more days of warm weather and the ice will be gone from Buffalo Lake. I'll be able to break the boat in and do a little crappie fishing and maybe catch some bass (ugh!). I might even be able to get in the Fox River and catch a few of those walleyes that came up earlier in March. This time of the year, everything pops as soon as the ice goes out. Northerns move into the shallows, the bass follow to feed on panfish, the crappies come in to eat minnows and walleyes move into the river to spawn all at the same time. It's hard to decide what to do, but I usually opt for the walleyes!

The boat looks great, and all the gizmos work on it. The boys down at Westpoint, Mississippi where the boat is made, did a great job on it. I'm chompin' at the bit to get it out on the water. I gotta believe that it's only a few days away. There's always something special about putting that first fish in the livewell of a new boat!

Easter Sunday, March 30th

The most special day of the year for Christians as we celebrate the Resurrection of our Saviour. Sherry and I volunteered for the nursery and have 24 kids from a few months up to three years old. Now I want to tell you, that's a long two hours! But it was kind of fun, at times. One little girl wanted to be held the whole time, so it was interesting trying to handle all the others with one arm. I think it helped get my casting arm in shape!

It was a great day of twofold rejoicing, however, as we celebrated Christ's Resurrection and the resurrection of spring. After church, I drove past the Fox River bridge and the river was clogged with ice from Buffalo Lake. That means the walleyes will be in the river tomorrow. Boy, I've been waiting about five months for this day! It's awesome to see the lakes opening up, and just getting keyed up to do some major fishing. It's also good to see the waterfowl coming back to the open marshes, the spring birds singing, and the promise that spring itself, is just around the corner. It looks like I'm going to get a good taste of it, before I get the full course meal down in Arkansas. This is kind of like the hors d' oerves before the banquet. I can't wait to get to Arkansas, get on the water, start prefishing and hopefully win the 1997 Super Pro event. I've been to Lake Ouachita before, and feel pretty confident about this tournament.

April 2nd

I spent the last couple of days putting the finishing touches on the boat and watching and waiting for the walleyes to show up in the river. A couple of my buddies said they caught a few yesterday, so I called up an old duck huntin' buddy of mine from Milwaukee, Jack DeMunck, and we went down river to the mouth of Lake Puckaway where we hunt ducks and I used to guide. It's a beautiful 63-degree day as we launch the boat and motor down river to the lake. There are ducks everywhere, inspiring us to talk about last fall's duck season.

Arriving at the mouth of the river, we discover that the lake is still frozen. That's okay, though, as we know some male walleyes have probably moved into the warmer river. We vertical jigged several of the river's deep holes before finally finding a small group of fish. It's amazing how a five-month layoff from fishing can make a guy so rusty. I had six bites and missed them all, before finally getting the hang of it and catching two. It wasn't a great day of

Chatting with Bob Propst before a seminar. There are many pros on the seminar circuit and they bump into each other often as they criss-cross the country.

catching, but a beautiful day of fishing. And I know that it's going to be a lot better tomorrow.

April 3rd

It's another 60-degree day, and another friend of mine, Bill Brooks and I went fishing on the Fox River where I always fished as a kid. After about an hour of kind of playing around with short bites and missing fish, I finally put it together and we ended up both taking a five-fish limit of walleyes. They were typical pre-spawn fish, mostly males, sitting right on the edge of the current in about four feet of water. We anchored the boat shallow in about two feet and cast 1/16th ounce Odd'Ball Jigs tipped with fathead minnows upstream into the current and let the current slowly move the jig downstream along the current edge, with just a little help by raising the rod tip and very slowly reeling up the slack. This has always been a deadly presentation for me, and one I've been using for almost 45 years.

I like casting jigs a lot better than vertical jigging and it gave me an opportunity to really test the new 5 1/2-foot walleye series jigging rod that I helped Quantum design. It's an excellent jigging

It's good to get out and fish as soon as the ice opens up an get the rust off my angling skills.

stick. I could really feel the bite and it handled the fish well. Boy, it's good to be fishing again!

Tonight I have a dinner meeting with Mike Phillips, Marketing Director for Mercury Marine. Mike has been a great friend over the years, and I appreciate his hard work in putting together my contract after Brunswick sold Fisher Boats to Tracker Marine. Mike has always bent over backwards for me, which isn't always a real common thing in the fishing industry.

April 4th

With a show coming up this weekend and a speaking engagement Monday night, you can bet I'm goin' fishing today! The temperature is a sunny, 75 degrees, which is about 30 degrees above normal for this time of year. The meeting with Mike went well, but I couldn't talk him into taking a day off to go fishing with me. In fact, I couldn't find anyone to go today, so I just had to enjoy catching all those walleyes myself. The water temperature shot up to an unbelievable 55 degrees, and the fish were really aggressive.

I used the same technique as yesterday, just drifting that jig right into the face of the fish. Except today, they were really slamming it!

I like casting jigs a lot better than vertical jigging and it gave me an opportunity to really test the new 5 1/2-foot walleye series jigging rod that I helped Quantum design.

Saturday, April 5th

I'm speaking at the Royal Ridges Sportshow in Ripon, Wisconsin today. It's a nasty day, with strong winds and rain, just the kind of day you want for a sportshow this time of year. The weather keeps people from working on their lawns and gardens. It even keeps anglers off the water, although if I wasn't at the show, I'd be fishin' for sure! There was a decent turnout at the show, but I think a lot of guys were out fishing. Like I always used to say, "I may not be able to work in this weather, but I can sure go fishing in it!" Steve Rose, author of *A Leap of Faith, God Must Be a Packer Fan,* was one of the other speakers and I had a good time visiting with him about his book and about the great Super Bowl year.

Sunday, April 6th

Right after church, Sherry and I blasted over to Ripon for another seminar I had to give in the afternoon. The weather has really turned ugly, with snow in the forecast for tonight. Oh, the joys of living up north! In fact, it's supposed to be downright cold all week, which will really give me an incentive to head to Arkansas on Thursday. My seminar today was sandwiched between Jeff Thomason, tight-end for the Packers, and Dan Small, host for the TV series, Outdoor Wisconsin. That's a really great time slot! As always, there was great interest in walleyes and what the change of weather would do to the bite. Almost as much interest as to whether the Packers would have another shot at the Super Bowl. Jeff Thomason proved to be a great guy, even though he doesn't fish (he's from California). And it was really great renewing my old friendship with Dan Small. Tomorrow night I speak at Manitowoc, Wisconsin at a couples' dinner, then run my taxes into the accountant, pack up the suburban and get ready for the long-awaited first tournament of the season.

1997 Super Pro
Lake Ouachita, Arkansas

Thursday, April 10th

Sherry and I are heading south on I-39 toward Arkansas with boat in tow! Fantastic! Last night we taught our church youth group which made me glad our own teenagers have grown up! I can't thank my wife, Sherry, enough for all her help in getting us ready not only for this trip, but for the hundred or so other trips the past few years. She has been a huge blessing and encouragement to me all along the way.

I finally got everything organized, the boat cover on and the truck loaded this morning, a little later start than I wanted. It took me at least two days to get everything together. The truck is loaded with at least 30 rods and reels, which is way too many. But you never know what you're going need. I've got every kind of Mann's crankbait known to man, and at least 50 pounds of jigs and every plastic body you can imagine. Tackle-wise, I should be more than ready

A big snow storm is predicted between Illinois and Missouri, and we're hoping we can beat it. It's hard to believe, after the nice weather, that we're going to get a snowstorm in southern Illinois on the 10th of April. That doesn't bode well for driving, especially towing a boat. But at least I'll be fishing south of it where the weather will be warmer and the fish biting! Lake Ouachita is about 950 miles from home, a 16-hour drive. With the late start, and possible bad roads, we're hoping to make at least half of that today.

Well, we made it to the Missouri border and it's snowing like a banshee. Cars and trucks are in the ditch everywhere, I'm in four-wheel drive and hoping to get south of St. Louis and drive out of this mess. I had hoped to get farther south than this, but am getting eye-weary from staring at the swirling snow.

The snow finally quit just south of St. Louis and we found a nice motel in a small town away from the city. There's about five inches of snow on the ground just to the north of us, and more predicted for tomorrow. I'm glad we left a day earlier than we really needed to. I hear there's a foot of it up where we live. Kind of glad I'm not guiding up there right now.

Friday, April 11

Well, we're on our way south and it's early in the morning. I noticed that my right taillight isn't working, which really is no surprise with several pounds of frozen slush hanging on the wiring.

Prefishing in the Arkansas sunshine sure feels good after a long winter. Pulling bottom bouncers along steep rocky bluffs like this turned out to be the winning pattern.

After trying to fix it with no success, I decided to just pull on out. It's getting light now, so I won't need it today. I'll just have to get it fixed before I leave for home in 10 days.

We pulled into Mountain Harbor Resort on beautiful Lake Ouachita just before sunset, and it looks just like it did when I was down here eight years ago doing a walleye fishing video for the Arkansas Department of Fish and Game. I only hope I can catch as many walleyes this week as I did back then! The weather is looking nice, but it's supposed to blow and turn pretty cold tonight. Doesn't that just figure. It could be worse, though. The place is packed with bass fishermen who qualified during the past season to fish the Champion Challenge, which starts tomorrow. You just know they're going to catch some big walleyes, and we'll end up catching lots of bass while prefishing tomorrow! I'm pumped up about hitting some of my old spots tomorrow and even the ominous weather forecast hasn't dampened my spirits.

Saturday, April 12, 1st day of practise

Okay. I said I couldn't wait. But it's 38 degrees, the wind is blowing 25 miles per hour out of the northwest and it is COLD! The only thing worse than trying to catch walleyes in this weather is fishing a bass tournament. I sure feel sorry for those guys! It might get up to 50 degrees today and tomorrow, so they say, and that's about normal temperatures back home this time of year. Well, I didn't come 950 miles to sit in the coffee shop. I might as well get out on the water and at least relearn the lake. Eight years is a long time to be away from a body of water.

The best pattern for southern reservoirs has been slow trolling with bottom bouncers and spinners tipped with night crawlers. I know that I'll eventually give it a try, but I've also done well with jigging spoons and jigs and half crawlers or minnows. I suspected that the fish would be deep with this cold front around, so I concentrated on deep ledges, casting and vertical jigging spoons. I had one big fish on that felt like a walleye, and caught several bass. I also spent a lot of time working the new weed growth, but with no success.

I'm not really discouraged, but I was hoping there'd be some fish in some of the places I knew about. Of course, with this big cold front, they could have been there, just not biting. That means I'll have to take another day of practice to re-fish those spots, something I don't like doing. But tomorrow's another day and I've got one creek arm I really want to work over, the south fork of the Ouachita River, where a lot of walleyes spawn. Maybe with the water being a cool 59 degrees, there will be some fish lingering up there, or at least at the mouth of it. I sure hope the wind settles down tonight. The forecast is for better weather later this week.

Sunday, April 13th

Well, I went up the south fork of the Ouachita River today, and man it looked good up there. The water was cleaner than the north fork with incredible structure and good shoreline points with deep water. I did a lot of jigging and ran some bottom bouncers and spinners. I jigged an awful lot of good points and caught several nice bass but no walleyes. I fished bottom bouncers and spinners off the breaks: more bass, big bluegills, but no walleyes. On the way back, I fished some deep rock at 42 feet and caught a 12-inch walleye, so I at least know there are some walleyes in the lake. This deep pattern has been a winner on Lake Cumberland, Kentucky, twice the past two years, so now I'm thinking of trashing the spoons and jigs and spending the rest of my prefishing time with spinners.

It was a long day, fishing from 7:00 a.m. to 6:30 p.m. and I'm pretty tired and slightly discouraged. But I talked to Ron Lindner at the dock and he said he had talked to several guys and none of them had fish today. I still think this cold front's got 'em really off. I'm beginning to question the number of walleyes in this lake, which is the typical response of most pros when their first couple of days of practice don't produce. But cold fronts can make fishing look bad in lakes that are full of walleyes, so maybe when this weather warms up, the bite will get better. Boy, I sure hope so!

Right now, it looks like it's going to be any easy tournament to win if a guy can get on some fish, and not necessarily a whole lot of fish. It could be a replay of the championship at Cumberland last year where it only took 16 pounds in three days to win it. That could happen here, but things can change in a hurry. Hopefully, I'm looking at a little better day tomorrow.

Monday, April 14th

I'm heading out on the lake with Darrell Taylor, an outdoor writer from Lake of the Ozarks in Missouri. I still haven't decided what I'm going to do today; I guess I'll just head out to the lake and see what I can find. It's warming up, and I'm hoping the fish will move shallow. Right now, it seems they are pretty deep. I guess we'll just try a lot of stuff and see if we can put some kind of pattern together.

Monday night

It was an interesting day. We fished from sunrise to sunset, 12 hours and managed to catch three walleye, two that were under the 15-inch size limit and one that weighed about two pounds. We caught all three pulling bottom bouncers and spinners in 24-29 feet along steep breaks, but I just couldn't put together a good pattern on them. Of course, where I caught the one weigh-fish is my number one spot so far for the tournament. That's not real encouraging! But I've got two more days of practice to put this pattern together, and since I've caught all four of my walleyes on spinners, I better stick with it.

My plan is to go down to the main lake tomorrow and spend the full day. I'm thinking that maybe the fish have all pretty much moved down there with the water level dropping. I need to pull myself out

Opening ceremonies at the Walleye Super Pro.

of that South Fork and really work the main lake. I've only seen three other tournament anglers the first three days, so they are all fishing somewhere, although there's an awful lot of whining about the bite. I think some fish will begin to move shallower now that the cold front has passed, but I'm going to work a few steep drops close to shore with spinners, just to see if this pattern will work in the main lake.

Tuesday Morning, April 15th

It's 6:30 in the morning, the sun is rising over a beautifully calm lake. It's one of those mornings where you look over a lake with great anticipation for the day of fishing that lies ahead. The forecast today is for calm winds with temperatures in the 70's. Now that's what I've been waiting for!

My fishing guest today is Bernie Barringer, coauthor of this book. I'm excited about getting out today, in spite of the way the fishing has been. One thing about a slow prefishing is that as I get closer to the tournament, I get more pumped up. That's how I feel today. We're going to spend the whole day in the main lake, and if that doesn't pan out, I'll be back in the South Fork tomorrow. I'm still convinced that those fish will go shallow, where they are easier to catch and a limit can be put in the boat real quick.

Tuesday night

Bernie caught the only weigh fish today. I caught one short one. We caught both on spinners deep off of sheer rock faces. That's two keepers and four short ones in four days of practice, all on spinners. Do I have a pattern going here? I wonder. We fished down by the Buckville area where a bite was rumored and over 20 guys were there, which is half the tournament field. The Super Pro is comprised of the top 40 all-time money-winners on the Professional Walleye Trail. It's an honor to be invited to fish this kickoff event each spring and would be great to win it, but I'm sure not on a winning pattern right now.

Rumors are flying that it's going to take 40 pounds to win, but I doubt it. If it does, I'm betting second place will be in the 20's. I've only got one more practise day to put it together and am starting to feel the pressure. I have a meeting with Quantum/MotorGuide in an hour and still have a lot of spinner snells to tie. The battery charger is hooked up and the boat is all gassed up for tomorrow, so at least that's done. I think I'll look at fishing some more high cliff faces tomorrow and pretty much scrap the shallow bite, even though I'm sure it can be won shallow, somewhere. A few guys have caught some four-pound class fish, and I know most of the field is now fishing spinners, so I better stick with that pattern. Right now, I'm not very confident in what I've found. But sometimes things can turn around quickly. With fishing, you just never know.

Wednesday, April 16th

I'm fishing this morning with Andy Conley who is director of research, development and sales for Browning Corporation. He can only be on the water until about 10 o'clock, so I'll be dropping him off and picking up Bernie to finish out the day. Since Andy and I could only fish a few hours, I went to the South Fork where I caught a few fish earlier in the week just to see if they were still there. They weren't.

I picked up Bernie at 10:00 and we blasted down the main lake toward the dam, dragging spinners and crawlers along every stretch of deep shoreline rock we could find, including where we caught the fish yesterday. No luck. Something weird is going on with this bite, and I just can't put my finger on it. Of course, I will by the end of the day tomorrow. I only hope that I can bag a few fish and still be in contention to win when the day is done. The big word for tomorrow is "cold front" and a big one. That could make for a long day for everyone. Sometimes, however, the wind blowing into certain spots can really trigger a bite. Walleyes are a funny fish, you just never know.

Rumors are flying that it's going to take 40 pounds to win, but I doubt it. If it does, I'm betting second place will be in the 20's. I've only got one more practise day to put it together and am starting to feel the pressure.

Sometimes a cold front can really turn the fish on in one part of the lake and totally shut them down in another. But overall, I would say that this cold front doesn't bode well for the first day of the tournament. We're looking at a low below freezing tonight. I'm not really terrified of the coldfront, in fact it could really equalize things.

I've only got a few good spots to fish, and my strategy is to hit those first and hope for the best.

Thursday, April 17th

It's the first day of the Dee Zee/Walleye Angler Super Pro Tournament and there's no breeze this morning, but it's chilly. The cold front that came through last night wasn't has severe as predicted; the wind died down only an hour or so after it passed. I doubt that it will affect the fishing all that much.

My amateur partner today is Harry Kumpula from Lincoln, Nebraska. He told me he likes to fish with bottom bouncers and spinners, which is good, because we'll probably be doing just that all day. The pre-tournament rumor is that three or four guys caught a limit of good fish yesterday, which isn't real encouraging for those of us who struggled during prefishing. But they don't weigh the fish caught yesterday, only today and the next two days, so I still believe it's anybody's ballgame.

Thumbs up! Optimism reigns as day one is about to begin.

Thursday evening

The first tournament day is over and there were 122 fish weighed in, which was a surprise to everyone. There was a real good early morning bite, with a lot of guys catching their fish by 8:30 and then nothing the rest of the day. We managed to put two fish in the boat right away and things looked real good, catching both before 8:00 o'clock, missing and losing a couple of others. Then nothing the rest of the day. You can't imagine how frustrating that is, with the two fish in the boat that early and the rest of the day to fish, and catching no more. Both our fish came out of 40 feet of water with two-ounce bottom bouncers and gold spinners and crawlers. The rest of the day was spent losing rigs in rocks and timber. I know I'll be up late tonight tying up new snells.

The leading weight is 15 pounds and we ended up with 3.19. Just a few more fish would have really helped. I need a really big day tomorrow to get back in this. My plan is to get back to the same spot right away and really vacuum the area with spinners. The thing I couldn't put my finger on prior to the tournament was that the bite was early and the fish have to be caught quickly. I might just work

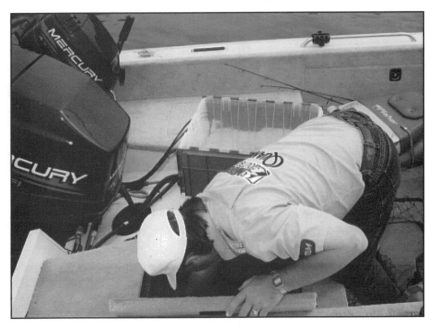

Sure would help if there was one more fish in here!

the spot until 8:30 or so, then spend the rest of the day trolling crankbaits, looking for a big fish. I might even go deeper, maybe out to 50 feet. Sometimes the larger fish are out there off of these steep breaks.

The big fish of the day was 4 1/2 pounds. That's not a really big fish for this system. In fact all of the biggest fish caught today were in that 4- to 4 1/2-pound class. That's a pretty good year class of females, but the Fish & Game Department says there is also a good class of 7- to 8-pound fish. I wonder if those fish are out in deeper water?

Sherry and I went to the Fellowship of Christian Anglers Society (FOCAS) meeting tonight. We had a real good turnout, about 22 people. It's always held the first night of the tournament and is a time of good fellowship and sharing of testimonies. For me, it helps keep things in perspective. Relationships and faith in Christ are more important than competition. That often can get lost during tournament time. I like that acronym, FOCAS. It reminds me to "focus" on my wife, my family, my friends.

The weather tonight is just beautiful as I sit outside tying snells

Chatting on stage with emcee Mike O'Rourke while day two partner Dave Patchett looks on.

for tomorrow. It's dead calm and a little cool. The sunset is simply gorgeous. If nothing else, it's really great to be down here this time of year, because the weather is still cold and nasty back home. Boy, I'm looking forward to getting back and getting some things organized for the next tournament at Dubuque. The river there hasn't crested yet and she's at flood stage now. It'll go above that somewhat and of course it'll begin to recede at some point, but I'm hoping it will remain high and stable by tournament time. I really hope it isn't dropping because that will make fishing really tough. Of course flood stage could be tough, too. High, dirty water would be okay for me, as I have done well there in the past under those conditions.

I can't believe I'm already looking ahead to the next tournament, with two more days to fish in this one. That kind of happens when you bomb on the first day, and things don't look all that much better for tomorrow. A limit of fish tomorrow would do wonders, however. It's just tough knowing that, without a miracle, I have no chance to win this tournament. So now the goal is to make the money cut. I have to forget about Dubuque right now and stay focused on the task at hand. I can be encouraged too, that some of the guys that limited today, never caught a fish in practise.

Friday, April 18th
My day two partner is Dave Patchett from Baxter, Minnesota. The weather is calm right now, but 20-m.p.h. winds are predicted. My plan hasn't changed overnight, and I've got a feeling that this is going to be a better day.

Friday night
It was an interesting day. I almost fished it perfectly, but made one dumb mistake. We caught three nice fish right off the bat, but the bite died by 8:30. We then went out trolling crankbaits off of a huge flat until noon, with no takers. Blasting back to our first spot, we caught a fourth fish right away and our hopes soared for a limit of five fish. But it wasn't to be. We should have stayed and worked that stretch all day, and I believe we would have taken a limit.

Dave and I ended up weighing just under nine pounds, which put me within a half-pound of the money cut. I need a good four- or five-fish day tomorrow to take home a decent check. Part of the day didn't go so well, as my main battery went down. I don't know how it happened, but something probably got left on or turned on and it drained during the night. I switched it over to my marine radio battery and it lasted the rest of the day, but I had to shut off the GPS and one locator and really baby the electricity I used. The main thing was to make sure the recirculator kept those fish alive! The engine barely turned over at 3:30 when I needed to head back, so right now I've got four battery chargers hooked up to four batteries so they'll all be charged and ready to go for tomorrow.

We went through another dozen bottom bouncers and spinners today, so I'll be spending a good couple of hours tying up new rigs tonight. I sure hope there's a few more fish on that spot tomorrow, but I'm a little uneasy about it. Maybe a good bunch will move up, and maybe I've caught all that was there. I just don't know. It's the kind of thing that keeps waking you up in the night.

Saturday, April 20th, Day Three

Another gorgeous morning with light winds and a beautiful sunrise. I didn't get much sleep last night thinking about that spot and where I would fish if it didn't pan out. I can definitely make a good check with only three fish. Anymore than that is a bonus for sure. It would be nice to at least cover my expenses for this trip, which will run about $2700. Tonight we're roasting PWT Executive Director, Jim Kalkofen for his 50th birthday. That should be fun. We'll then catch a few hours of sleep and try to make the 950-mile drive straight through on Sunday. But first, down to business.

Saturday evening

The 1997 Walleye Super Pro is history and I had a disappointing day. I ended up catching one fish at 3:30 this afternoon and had time to make one more pass, losing a good fish before heading in. I ended up 25th overall and could have easily made the money with one more decent fish in the boat. My friend, Chad Hall won the tournament, fishing the exact same pattern that I was fishing. The only difference is that he worked a little bit shallower than I did, staying at about 24 feet. This was his third PWT win, all on spinners. He certainly knows his stuff.

My best spot bombed out and I probably stayed there way too long, but I was just hoping that a bite would happen at some point during the day on that spot. It didn't. I ended up catching my only fish at the spot where I lost that good fish the first day of practise. In retrospect, I could have done a few things different to finish higher than I did. First of all, I should have stayed on my first spot longer on day-one and day-two. I'm sure I would have taken a few more fish. Secondly, I should have moved to the first break, which was 24 feet, instead of continuing to fish the second break at 40-45 feet. Tournament fishing is all about learning, no matter how many tournaments you've fished. I learned a great lesson here, and though I know that I could have done better, it's time to move on to the next event. The word is Dubuque is at flood stage and muddy. That means the fish will be tucked in shallow, my favorite kind of bite. Of course that's three weeks away and a lot can happen by then.

The Kalkofen roast was a riot, with many of the pros staying after the tournament to participate. The Glorvigon twins emceed the event and taped Jim's mouth shut so he couldn't talk. Everyone agreed that it was a good idea. Jim took it really well, though, and Sherry and I were glad we stayed. Jim and his wife, Marsha, have been great friends of ours for many years. It was fun to help him celebrate his 50 years.

Monday, April 21

We managed to make the drive straight through, and after resting for a day, went through 12 days of mail and phone messages, which took us all day. Wednesday I'll be fishing with a student from nearby Princeton High School for a job shadow day. I wish I could have talked my teacher into THAT when I was a kid!

Wednesday, April 23

Reality check! It's in the 20s right now as Todd Ruhl, a high school senior and I head out to Lake Puckaway to try some bass fishing. My plan is to get some good shots of Todd holding up some largemouth and smallmouth bass for the camera; shots I'll need for the upcoming issues of the Marquette and Green Lake County Guides that Sherry and I help publish. The water's a little cold, only in the low 50's, but the smallies should bite at least, and maybe as the sun warms up the shallows, we can stick a couple of largemouths.

Todd also has to interview me for his class after we get off the water, so I'm not only trying to put him on some fish, but also articulate the intricacies of professional fishing. Should be interesting.

Wednesday night

In spite of the cold water, Todd and I had a pretty good day. I got the shots I needed for the guides, and I know that Todd learned quite a bit about early season bass fishing, cold front conditions and so on. He caught a 4-pound smallie, a nice photo fish; it will look good in one of the guides.

I really had fun, and look forward to doing more of that with kids. I think it's just so important to be able to take some kids out fishing and get 'em cranked up about it. Todd said his goal is to become a professional fisherman someday and it was good to be able to share with him the things that are involved with professional angling.

He has a vision and a dream, just like I had when I was his age. Some people might laugh at that, but I believe that dreams can come true if you want them bad enough, and that's what I tried to instill in Todd. This young man can fish, he learns fast and I have high hopes for his success.

Friday, April 25th

Today I met my son, Steve, at Rainbow Park in Oshkosh on the Fox River. The river was stacked with post-spawn walleyes and we had a great day together just catching fish for fun, and catching up on life.

Sunday, April 27th

When you're a full-time professional angler, it seems the seminars are never done. Right after church, I drove the 50 miles to Stevens Point to do a class at the Walleye College, directed by Jeff Taege, who fishes the circuit as well. It was well attended with strong interest in walleye fishing. I've got four days coming up to get my quarterly reports in to my sponsors before I head to Dubuque. The water's still high and muddy. I hope it stays that way.

Central Pro/Am, Mississippi River Dubuque, Iowa

Friday, May 2nd

The boat's hooked up and the rain's pourin' down as Sherry and I begin the three-hour drive to the Mississippi River. Our plan is to drive north to the tournament boundary and take a look at the water level there, then head down to Dubuque. This rain could bring the water back up, or at least stabilize it and that would make for a good bite. Falling water, on the other hand, could be a disaster.

The water level at the border proved to be high, but fairly clear, which was a real surprise. Even more surprising was that the water at Dubuque was cleaner than I had expected and falling fast, and that it could be within its banks by tournament time in six days. That could make for a decent bite, but the barge traffic is due to start any day, which would dirty up the water and change everything. I'm a little uneasy about the tournament already, because I know that in this one, I might have to throw the prefishing right out the window come tournament day.

Saturday, May 3rd

It's the first day of practise and not the kind of day I would want to fish for fun. The wind is 25 miles per hour out of the northwest and the air temperature is only 44 degrees. But I'm up and ready to go, having a warm breakfast at Country Kitchen and plenty of coffee. I bought my license and bait yesterday (leeches at $22 per pound) and a bunch of crawlers. In spite of the wind, I'm anxious to head down river and fish some of my old spots where I last fished here six years ago. I had planned to fish up river today, but don't relish the thought of a 30-mile run against a nine-mile an hour current and 25-30 mile per hour winds. Add to that lots of trees, stumps and other debris in the water, and it makes for a long, cold ride. So I'll head on down river to some of my old spots and see what I can find.

Saturday evening

The river is high and muddy, not as clean as it looked yesterday. I did manage to find some clean water in a back channel and caught a 3-pounder and a short one. There were five or six other tournament anglers there as well, all with local fishermen. That was really disappointing, as I had expected to have this spot pretty much to myself. I left the spot early and tried everything else I knew from there to the boat landing, with not even a bite. It was another one of those sunrise to sunset days of practise and I'm pretty tired.

I caught my two fish on 1/8th-ounce Odd'Ball Jigs tipped with leeches, casting to the bank and jigging out to deeper water. These channels should have been holding a lot more fish, but the one I

There were good numbers of fish in the back channels and harbors during prefishing, but too many anglers were beginning to learn the pattern.

fished today was getting quite a bit of pressure. I talked to some local guys tonight, and they said that particular channel was putting out a ton of walleyes about a week ago, so I suppose they're pretty well cleaned out. I also talked to a few fishermen that I can trust, and they said they did really well in the upper pool where the water is cleaner. I may have to spend the next three days up there. We'll see.

Sunday, May 4th

It's still dark and I grab a box of donuts and a cup of coffee from the gas station and begin the drive to the upper pool. I try to launch at the main ramp, but can't get in as the high water is still in the parking lot. My map shows another ramp down river and just as I'm leaving, I run into Bill Ortiz, one of our top anglers, and he directs me to the other ramp. It was an iffy launch, but I got in okay.

The river is way cleaner here. I can see a jig down about a foot, as opposed to one inch in the lower pool. Making my way to dam, I'm surprised at the number of boats already up there. In fact, it's bumper boats. Guys are jerking out small sauger by the hundreds, but I don't think this sauger bite is going to do it. My guess is that a six-fish daily tournament limit from here would weigh maybe six to seven pounds. Of course, that could make the money if the tournament is tough.

I opt to move downstream and find several good eddies and channel cuts that should be holding walleyes. I finally catch one fish about five pounds, but that's it for the day. Man, I fished an awful lot of good looking stuff. Where are these fish? All of the gates at the Guttenburg dam were wide open, with trees and other stuff coming through. If guy could motor right through the dam if he wanted to, but it is highly illegal to do so. With all that water coming down, I don't expect the water to drop too much down below. Maybe I should look for more channels down there and if I can find enough spots, cherry-pick them during the tournament. A limit of fish of any size here would win the tournament. I hope I'm not giving up on the upper pool too soon.

Monday, May 5th

Just like it always snows in Green Bay, I think it always rains in Iowa. The rain's coming down in buckets and the wind is gusting at 40 miles per hour. The weather service says it's going to quit within the hour, so I'm having breakfast and coffee at the Julian Inn with a whole bunch of other anglers, all of whom claim to have caught only one or two fish in two days. If they're telling the truth, then all of us are in the same boat and I need to work harder than ever to put this together. Looking out the restaurant window, I see mudflats that weren't here two days ago, which means the water is dropping faster than I thought it would. That means the current is going to be running slower and the wing dams, which are traditionally good walleye spots, could become fishable by tournament time.

I'm sitting in my truck with the heater running and rain drenching the parking lot of the boat ramp. Only one boat has launched so far and it's already 8:00 a.m. Normally I've got an hour of fishing in by now. That means I'll be fishing until dark, because I don't like losing prefishing time. I think I'll buzz down to Catfish Creek where I won the tournament in '88. I expect this to get pounded, but it's a good backup spot.

Monday night

I finally made a good decision today and fished a couple more back channels, catching a limit of weigh fish in only a few hours. I didn't see many guys out, and I'm hoping that most of them aren't on this pattern, or have already given it up because it wasn't that good the first day. The wind kind of forced me to fish tight to shore, but I still had to quit at 3:00 as there was no way to control the boat, even in the protected areas. Every channel did have a few guys in it, but most were vertical jigging the deep channel, while I was casting toward shore. Two of my fish came out of a foot of water. With what I caught today, there's no way I'm going back up to the upper pool. If I can just find a couple of backup spots down here in case the bite goes sour or it gets too crowded in the channels, I'll be okay.

Tuesday, May 6th

It's a bright, sunny and calm morning and I'm hoping that the weather will influence most of the guys to run to the upper pool today. I'm fishing with Bob Henry today, an Iowan who has fished the river before. My hope is to maybe fish some wingdams today, since they haven't been getting fished real hard.

Tuesday night

It's 6:15 and we just got off the water. We tried to fish wingdams but the current was still too strong. The mouth of Catfish Creek had at least 20 boats on it at any given time today. Guys must really be struggling. I was surprised and disappointed at the number of anglers working the harbors and channels today. The word must be out on the small bite going on. While most are vertical jigging, a few of the guys who are good at casting jigs were there also. Not a good sign. I decided to go down to where I caught the fish the first practise day and there were only a few guys there. We caught a limit right away, so I got out of there before anyone saw me. Unfortunately, as I came out, I was greeted by an entourage of boats coming in.

Our next stop was the Ice Harbor, where I missed three fish, but was encouraged that there were a few walleyes in there. I hadn't seen anyone fishing in there all week but Harry Stiles, a good jigger, who came in as I was going out. He had a concerned look on his face, so I assumed he had been working this area. Another channel produced two more fish, and I was beginning to feel that this could be good.

These back channels have been dug out for marinas, so there is a deep channel with steep sides. Often the walleyes will be right on the edge, and sometimes out deep. Since the water is fairly clear, you have to cast to the shore and bring the jig off the edge. Vertical jigging works best for the deeper fish. It's real similar to bass fishing, and we found walleyes to be hanging close to and even under moored boats, as well as around some of the old pilings. But would there be enough to go around for everyone? Probably not.

Bernie Barringer arrived this evening with the good news that he and his son, Ben had been fishing farther down river and Ben caught a 7-pounder trolling crankbaits. Ouch! The last thing I wanted

I finally made a good decision today and fished a couple of more back channels, catching a limit of weigh fish in only a few hours. I didn't see many guys out, and I'm hoping that most of them aren't on this pattern, or have already given it up because it wasn't that good the first day.

to hear with one day of practise to go is that a crankbait bite was starting. My hope is that it was a rogue walleye and that no pattern exists. At least they didn't catch a boatload of them. Of course, if they had, I would be trolling crankbaits tomorrow!

There's an old saying out there that says "ya gotta dance with the chick that brought ya", and that's my plan in this one. With only one short day of practise to go, I'm going to try to find at least one more spot to fall back on. The water is still almost five feet above normal and I'm hoping it's enough to hold the fish in the channels, or even move some new fish in there. These channels and harbors are full of shad, another reason the walleyes have moved in. If the shad stay, the walleyes should stay.

Wednesday, May 7th

It's the last day of practise and I really wish practise would have ended a couple of days ago. More and more guys are on the channel patterns now and I know it's going to be crowded. I'm fishing with Bernie and Ben today and filming a TV slot for Fox. I didn't promise the TV guy anything, especially not footage of walleyes being

Television interviews are important. Even during the stress and pressure of prefishing, they must be done.

caught. The guy was anxious because it was spitting a little rain, and high winds and heavy thunderstorms are predicted both today and for the first day of the tournament tomorrow.

Wednesday evening

Sometimes things work out in weird ways. We decided to motor across the river into a calm area to do the filming. It was a spot I had fished several years ago in the MWC Championship, a railroad bed riprap area. With the cameras rolling, rain falling, and me hyping up the tournament and talking about the tough bite, Bernie tosses a jig in and whacks a 6-pound walleye. Did I ever look like a hero on the local news at 6:00 and 10:00! Just about every one of the tournament guys saw it and were pumping me for info at the rules meeting. If nothing else, I put some fear into the hearts of a lot of guys with that fish.

With the cameras rolling, rain falling, and me hyping up the tournament and talking about the tough bite, Bernie tosses a jig in and whacks a 6-pound walleye. Did I ever look like a hero on the local news at 6 and 10!

The Fox guys got some great footage and were really excited to get it done. The first of several thundershowers hit just as they were loading their gear back in the truck. And so the day went. Thunderstorms and torrential rain. We didn't catch another fish all morning and by one o'clock were soaked to the skin, even with rain gear. I brought Bernie and Ben back to their car, and just sat in my boat in the parking lot, in the rain, tying jigs on six jigging rods for tomorrow's fishing. With that finished, it was time to hook up the chargers and take my wet clothes in to dry. By the sound of the forecast, I was going to need them again tomorrow.

The rules meeting is held the last night of practise. It's when we find out who our three amateurs are for the three days of the tournament. The In-Fisherman Professional Walleye Trail (PWT) is a pro-am circuit, but it is quite different in that the pro and amateur fish as partners, instead of against one another and weigh their "boat weight" each day. For example, on day one, we weigh six fish that total 20 pounds, both of us get 20 pounds. That weight then carries over into the next day of competition. Then say, he and his second day partner catch 30 pounds and me and my second day partner catch 20 pounds again. My first day partner now has 50 pounds, while I have 40 pounds. The same thing goes on day three. So often the amateur winning weight is higher than the pro division because of who he fished with each of the three days.

We really like this format because it encourages us to teach our partner as much as we can, since his catch helps us out. The amateurs like it as well, because they get to learn a lot about walleye fishing from three different pros, plus they can go back and brag to their buddies that they helped the pro win the tournament.

Since it's a draw format, we never know who our amateur partners will be until the night of the rules meeting. The skill level of amateurs runs the gambit from beginner to guys who are good enough to fish as pros. In fact, several of the touring pros today formerly fished as amateurs. The PWT is invitational only on the pro side, with the top 100, based on last year's total weight for four qualifiers being invited to fish. Next year, that field might be reduced even

Staging for the take-off in the flooded Mississippi backwaters.

further. The remaining slots, up to 120, are filled with rookies and sometimes veterans who had to drop out a year or two for business or personal reasons.

Tournament Director and friend, Mark Dorn, told me that if I can catch a limit each day and get a "kicker" (a big fish) or two, I'll probably win. Right now, if I can fish my spots and the water level doesn't drop too fast, I think I can do it. In fact, I feel pretty confident that this is a winnable tournament for me. My goal is to catch a limit the first day and see where I'm at, because they're predicting (what else) a major cold front for Friday and Saturday.

I'm ready to go mechanics-wise, and mentally, I feel strong. I only wish I had a couple of spots to myself, but that probably won't happen, so I'm going to have to be patient, work the water, fish slower than the other guys, and pick apart those back channels. If I do all of those things, I should be able to take a limit of fish..

Thursday, May 8th, Day One

My partner today is Herb Franks from Marengo, Illinois. Herb has fished as an amateur for several years and has said he always wanted to draw me. He is very excited, especially after I told him I was catching fish. The weather is actually warm and winds calm right now with a little fog. The rain has stopped, but Herb has his rain gear on which is bright chartreuse! A great jig color for sure, but it won't be easy to hide from anybody today.

I decided to hit the spot I fished the first day of practice and caught that three-pounder. There were four boats in the cut to get into the channel when I got there, and three more in the channel. Herb and I slid around them and went to the back end where I had caught that fish the first day. On the second cast, I caught one about 16-inches and boy were we excited. We worked the area hard, but caught nothing else. We then worked our way back out to the slot, and the crowd was now 12 boats in a spot big enough for two. I slid down away from the group and caught another small fish. It was only nine o'clock and I felt good that we could catch a limit today.

We stayed in the channel until 10:30, then headed back upstream to fish another channel. There was a good crowd at Catfish Creek, about 20 boats, as we went by. "We're not stopping here," I told Herb, even though a few of the boats had their livewells running and one was netting a fish. We motored up to the next cut and there were four boats in the one-boat spot. I decided to pass it and go up to the Ice Harbor.

Harry Stiles was motoring out as I was coming in, and he just shook his head, meaning the bite was tough. I was dying to ask him what he caught, but we're not allowed to share information during tournament hours. I didn't notice if his livewell was running. Since we had the harbor all to ourselves, I decided to really vacuum the shoreline with jigs and leeches, hoping to scrounge out at least a couple of fish. It didn't happen.

Our two fish for the day weighed 2.90 pounds and it doesn't bode well for the rest of the tournament. There were 47 zeroes and another 50 anglers had only one fish. With my two, I'm sitting a half-pound out of the money in 32nd place.

Friday, May 9th, Day Two

My partner today is James McDowell from Burstall, Saskatchewan. James is retired and he's fishing the PWT for the first time. He said he was hoping to draw somebody today that would put him on some fish. We both kind of laughed and my somber attitude about the day began to change.

Why do weather forecasters always have to be right when you don't want them to be? The predicted cold front slammed in with vigor during the night with wind chills right now in the 20's and temperature at 43 degrees. They're talking big wind by this afternoon, but since we're on the river, we should be pretty protected. I'm glad I'm not running north to the other pool, even though I know the first day leader, Chris Gilman, is fishing up there.

When you only catch two fish the first day, and you really have nothing else going, you head back to the same spot. It was a cold ride down the river, and being in the last flight, I expected to find a lot of boats in the channel. Catfish Creek now had at least 50-60 boats—an indication that some fish were caught there yesterday. I refuse to participate in that mess, I don't care how many fish are there.

I decided to modify my approach today, holding the boat out in a little deeper water, and having James vertical jig while I cast to the shallows. My thought is that the cold front might have pushed the fish a little deeper, since these channels and harbors are quite similar to fishing small lakes. Since I'm in the third flight today and it's my long day, I'm hoping to have more time to really work my spots.

We went straight to where I caught the fish yesterday and had a

15-incher right off the bat. Maybe, just maybe, this is going to be my day. It wasn't. I ended up losing four fish today, which you just can't do on a tough bite. I'm mystified. I never lose fish like that, especially shallow jig fish. I don't get it. More fish were weigh in today, thanks to the boat pack at Catfish Creek. More boats, more fish caught; a pretty common thing. I hate to see how many boats will be there tomorrow with it being a Saturday and the local folks out fishing as well. I know one who WON'T be there!

The wind just howled all day today and it's still blowing 25 mph out of the northwest. We had our advisory council meeting tonight and I was elected to serve on it for the fifth time in eight years and the third year in a row. It's really an honor that your peers elect you

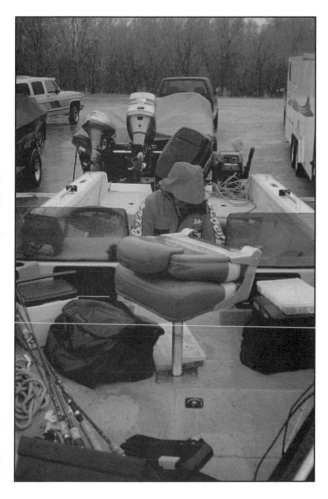

Even though it's pouring rain, rods need to be rigged, battery chargers need to be hooked up and the boat needs to be organized. Some days these tasks are not very pleasant.

to this post. We work closely with the PWT directors to address the anglers concerns, as well as those of management. Many good rules have resulted from these meetings, as well as a few of the not-so-good rules thrown out.

Chris Gilman was still leading the tournament. In fact he's so far ahead that he probably doesn't even need to go out tomorrow. It would probably be a good idea if he did, however. Right now, I'm not sure of my game plan, except, I'll most likely go back to where I caught my three fish, work it quickly and try some wingdams. I'm pretty bummed and really tired from all the wind, the advisory council meeting running late, and the disappointment of not catching more fish. The good news is that I'm not out of this yet, and a limit would at least put me in the money.

Saturday, May 10th

Chris Speiker, a young man from Chicago is my day three partner. He's excited and looks like a real good fisherman. Hope I can show him something today. He had a good day yesterday, and is

The fish were in the back channels and harbors, too, but there were not enough to go around. The pattern was fading and many anglers were chipping away at their numbers.

poised to finish well. I want to help him out, and we're going to fish hard, for sure. Since it's my short day, it's down to the harbor, fish it quick and shotgun every spot I caught fish in practise and during the tournament. Then, time permitting, work some of the best wingdams.

Saturday evening

Another one-fish day. We fished our game plan to the max, but managed to take only one fish from an empty harbor. The reason it was empty was that Catfish Creek now had about 80-90 boats on it. Without sounding to sanctimonious, that's pretty pathetic. I mean, from 20 boats on day one? Get real. What's amazing is that some of the guys actually took limits of fish from that mess. That has never been and never will be my kind of fishing. If I was an amateur and got stuck fishing that way, I'd be pretty disappointed.

Although my philosophy is: "don't leave fish to go to fish", it's often difficult to stay when they're not biting. Another lesson learned.

The good news is that Chris Gilman won with 25 pounds. As it turned out, he needed to catch his one and only fish on day three to squeak past Mark Martin who had 24 pounds. Both Chris and Mark were fishing away from others. That's how you win tournaments, not fishing next to 80 other boats.

Another bit of disturbing news was that the harbor I started at turned on at about 11 o'clock and all six boats caught a limit. Add to that fact two limits were taken there on day two, again around 11 o'clock, and I realized that I probably should have stayed in that channel for the whole tournament. But how does a guy know? That's all part of the tournament scene, and although my philosophy is: "don't leave fish to go to fish," it's often difficult to stay when they're not biting. Another lesson learned. That's two lessons in two tournaments. It would be nice to teach some of my peers a lesson or two down the road!

Anyway, thanks guys for the fishin' lessons. As long as I can continue to learn something from each tournament, it makes it all worthwhile fishing in them. Fortunately, I don't have to win to keep

Often there's a few days of guiding to be done between tournaments.

things going, thanks to my great sponsors, Mercury Marine, Fisher Boats, Quantum/MotorGuide, Wille Products, Bait Rigs Tackle, Mustad Hooks, Stren Fishing Lines and Mann's Baits. They not only help pay for it all, but they provide me with the best equipment and tackle money can buy.

Monday, May 12th

It isn't often that a guy gets much time off in between tournaments, but I've got about two weeks to get ready for the next qualifier. Actually, I'm mentally ready right now and wish the tournament was this week, but not Sherry. As usual it's catchup time and will take a few days to sort out mail and answer phone calls. I also have five days of guiding booked in, so time will go fast before heading to Leech Lake, Minnesota.

Midwest Pro/Am
Leech Lake
Walker, Minnesota

Tuesday, May 27th

Boy, that went fast. Sherry and I are heading up I-94 toward Leech Lake, the second stop on the PWT. We finally got a break in the weather after a mighty cold spring. In fact, the ice went off of Leech only a few days ago, so I expect the water to be pretty cold. It's only a short, eight-hour drive to Leech, although we'll be taking the long way, because I want to stop at the Bait Box in Superior, Wisconsin to get some bait.

We picked up three pounds of leeches at the Bait Box, only $9 per pound, which was a little cheaper than Dubuque. I also replaced my spinner components and quick change cleavices that I lost at the Super Pro. Tony Puccio from Bait Rigs will be loading me up with spinners and bottom bouncers when I get there. My hope is for a shallow jig bite, but I'm guessing spinners or Lindy Rigs fished deep will take the bigger fish.

My bill came to $43.26 for the bait and tackle, but I'm set for prefishing. I might, however, load up on some nice shiners when I get closer to Leech Lake and I probably should consider getting six dozen crawlers right away, so I have plenty of bait to start practice. Usually a guy can get good bait right in Walker, but I hate to take any chances. Besides, I have to pick up a Minnesota license anyway, so I might just as well load up on bait.

Tuesday evening

We pulled into Walker, Minnesota at Leech Lake around 2:30 this afternoon, making great time. At this particular tournament we had our boats inspected for zebra mussels and Eurasian milfoil. The check went quickly, and my boat was cleared to fish. I spent the rest of the day getting rods rigged and replacing line as well as cleaning up the boat. It took a surprising five hours, but I'm fired up and ready to go. The lake is simply beautiful, with loons calling at sunset and the great northwoods all around. I'll sleep like a baby tonight.

Wednesday, May 28th

Today was my first time fishing on Leech Lake, not counting bass fishing with Ron Lindner a few years back, or ice fishing with Al Lindner two years ago. It was my first time fishing walleyes in open water and I really enjoyed it. The lake seems smaller than it really is (113,000 acres) and there is a chain of lakes attached to it. Rumor says the tournament will be won in Walker Bay where the fish tend to run larger. So I checked that out first, then the narrows between the bay and the main lake.

Walker Bay proved interesting with its many deep water humps. The bay itself is 156 feet deep with many humps that top off at 24 feet. Walleyes congregate on these humps in late spring, but I didn't mark or catch any fish on them.

The cut between the bay and main lake was loaded with fish, especially where the new cabbage weed was sprouting. I caught several fish there today, simply casting a Slo-Poke Jig and leech into the short weeds and jigging it back. Most of the fish came from four to six feet of water, with a few off the edge in 11 feet. My biggest was three pounds, which I caught casting a jigging spoon off of a rock hump.

I noticed that the fish I was catching in the weeds were coughing up small crayfish, so I'm going to try some orange jigs tomorrow and see if I can take some bigger fish. As it stands right now, I'm pretty impressed with the bite on Leech Lake. But first impressions aren't always what they seem to be.

During our five prefishing days, the Chamber of Commerce has organized a sporting clays event, with a point system that includes our tournament finish. I participated in the shoot this afternoon and had fun, but didn't do all that well, breaking only 12 of 25, about average for the rest of the guys in my group. Dale Dykes, a friend of mine from Iowa, was in my group shooting sporting clays for the first time. He started out slow, but ended up breaking 13. He had a blast. Rick LaCourse won the event, breaking 23 of 25, which was incredible, since the course was so tough. I later found out that he had designed this particular course and shoots sporting clays all the time.

Following the event, we were treated to barbecued buffalo and smoked salmon from Ketchikan, Alaska. It's what my wife calls "man food". It was really good stuff! The fishermen were all in good spirits being up in this wonderful country. It's spring, the birds are singing, there's not muddy water and the wind is yet to blow. I'm really looking forward to tomorrow and fine-tuning my pattern.

Thursday, May 29th

It's our 26th wedding anniversary today, and we're celebrating by going out for breakfast at 5:30 a.m. Now that's a great wife for you! I'll be fishing with Wesley Brooks from the Twin Cities today. Right now the weather is overcast with light winds and the smell of rain in the air. It should be a good fishing day, although Gary Roach told me that the bite can get really bad on Leech Lake if we don't get any wind. We'll see.

I noticed that the fish I was catching in the weeds were coughing up small crayfish, so I'm going to try some orange jigs tomorrow and see if I can take some bigger fish. As it stands right now, I'm pretty impressed with the bite on Leech Lake.

My plan is for both of us to cast jigs shallow all day, and work some other weed beds that I've marked on my map. I plan to fish long today to make up for taking off a little early yesterday. Tonight is advisory council meeting night as well, so I know I won't get to bed until after 10:00. That makes for a long day.

Thursday night

Roach was right. No wind, no fish. Well actually, we caught plenty of walleyes, but they were all short. Wes cast a jig and leech, while I cast jigging spoons. I caught over a dozen walleyes on the spoons, and Wes caught as many on jigs, but no size. I'm not giving up on this shallow pattern, yet. But I'm already thinking that the bigger fish might be out in deeper water. Arggghhhhh! I hate fishing deep water in spring. Tomorrow I'm fishing with Dave Csanda, editor of the *Walleye In-Sider* Magazine and a special friend. Dave and I have yet to catch any fish together, even though we've fished together every year. I'm not so sure if tomorrow's going to be that great. In fact, Dave suggested I not fish with him, like he's some kind of jinx or something.

Friday, May 30th

Dave, you are a jinx. We fished all day and once again, caught only short fish. It was a beautiful day, but calm as could be. I never thought I would say this, but COME ON WIND! I talked with a lot of guys tonight and the story seems to be the same. Although one guy did catch a few nice fish out in 17 feet of water on Lindy Rigs and minnows. Might have to give that a try tomorrow.

Saturday, May 31st

I'm fishing a mini-tournament today against five other guys with a first prize of $1,000 and last prize of $400. So at least I'm going to cash a check today. The forecast is for no wind and 82 degrees, which should give everybody a great tan.

Saturday evening

Amazing. I knew that if I could just catch one fish today, I'd make a little extra money. That I did, with a huge 1 1/2-pounder that put me in third place. I made 600 bucks for that and also won a battery charger for catching the biggest perch. I want to tell you, I've worked a lot harder in tournaments for a lot less money. The good news is that I caught the fish in a new spot. The bad news is that it's as far from the takeoff as you can get. The other bad news is that I caught the fish on a jigging spoon. One fish is not a pattern, even though I think, under the right conditions, spoons would work very well on Leech Lake. It was dead calm and 84 degrees today, not my ideal conditions.

Sunday, June 1st

It's 5:00 a.m. and the sun is coming up with no hint of wind. I'm getting an early start today, and should be on the water in a few minutes. I stopped at the bait shop and bought some good shiners at four bucks a scoop and stuck $18 worth of gas in the boat, same as yesterday. So at least I know how much gas I'll be using during the tournament. I'm planning to fish deeper today, but also give some of my shallow spots one last try. We have to be off the water by four o'clock the day before the tournament, so it's going to be a short day of practise.

Sunday night

Practise is over and we finally got the long-awaited wind everyone was hoping for. It didn't do much for the bite however, at least not where I was fishing. The consensus was pretty much the same with everyone else I talked to as well. I fished deep off of Stoney Point and caught a 23 1/2-incher as well as one just over 15. Guess where I'm starting tomorrow!

My plan is to work that area for several hours tomorrow and hopefully get some fish in the boat. The spot isn't too far from Ottertail Point and the next point down where I caught a couple of weigh fish in practise. At least I've shrunk the lake down in size a little bit.

I shot a commercial for Stren Fishing Line when I got back to the dock this afternoon. It will air on TNN during the In-Fisherman shows sometime this fall. There was a lot of whining about the bite at the rules meeting tonight, which means I'm not the only one that's struggling out there. The weird thing is, I know this lake is loaded with walleyes. Why can't we put this bite together? I don't think I ever worked as hard as I did the past four days, or have ever been as tired. It's only 8:30 and I'm ready to crash.

The good news is that I caught the fish in a new spot. The bad news is that it's as far from the take-off as you can get. The other bad news is that I caught the fish on a jigging spoon. One fish is not a pattern, even though I think, under the right conditions, spoons would work very well on Leech Lake.

Monday, June 2nd

It's Day One of the Western Pro-Am on Leech Lake. It seems really weird to start a tournament on a Monday, but the PWT scheduled it this way to avoid conflict with the Mercury Nationals which is this coming weekend. My partner today is Paul Kartaly from Altoona, Wisconsin, he seems like a nice guy and knowledgeable fisherman. The forecast is for sunny, calm and 85 degrees. I'm betting there won't be a whole lot of fish caught.

Monday night

I was right—130 boats caught only 144 fish and 31 zeroed including me. In fact there were only three limits caught, and the majority of the fish came from Ottertail point when the wind blew for about an hour. We fished Stoney for a long time, and could see the boats running all over the lake—a good indiction that the bite wasn't too good. But several stopped at Ottertail, which meant one of two things, either fish were being caught, or boats were begetting boats. The sunny and 85 turned into cloudy and rainy most of the day. There should have been a better bite. Most of us are missing it. My old friend, Gary Roach is the first day leader with 18 pounds. He's going to be tough to beat.

I did get an on-the-water interview with Channel 12 which aired at 6:00 and 10:00. We didn't have any fish at the time, so I just talked about the great hospitality we experienced in Walker and expressed optimism that the fish would turn on. Paul and I ended up catching 14 walleyes, none of which measured. The FOCAS meeting was tonight and I was the guest speaker. It was held from the PWT stage and there was a real good turnout even though it was spittin' rain.

Tuesday, June 3rd

It's 4:30 a.m. and I'm getting ready to launch the boat and go have some breakfast. It's been a tournament ritual for me, Scott Hauge, Steve Fellegy and Chad Hall to be the first to launch in the morning so we can get the best spots on the dock, as well as closest parking spots. A lot of guys laugh about that, but most places we fish have limited dock space, and the guys end up bobbing around in their boats for over an hour before takeoff, and that's no fun. And it sure is nice to be able to pull up at the end of the day and have the truck and trailer right by the ramp. Once the boat's in the water, we all head off for a good breakfast, which is really important before a long day on the water.

Sherry usually helps me launch, then we have breakfast together. I then meet my partner between 6:00 and 6:30 at the tournament headquarters, load his gear in the boat, get to know him a little better and do any last minute rigging. Next, we go over how to start and drive the boat in case I fall out or am unable to drive for some reason. We also go over emergency procedures, especially on Lake Erie and Saginaw Bay. Sherry then takes a photo of us together, which she mails to him after we get home. My partner today is Tim Herink from Plainfield, Illinois.

The forecast for today is little or no wind, but the locals say, with the warmer weather, the bite should improve. We'll see. Right now, after four tournament days, counting Dubuque, I'm only eight pounds

Mixed emotions characterize the feelings at the opening ceremonies. Will the wind blow and get these fish going at last?

out of qualifying for the championship. I'd like to chip away at that before heading over to Lake St. Clair where the weights are supposed to be pretty big. Since the fish weren't at Stoney yesterday, my plan is to run back there and work it for a short time, then go to the next point north of Ottertail. Hopefully some of those Ottertail fish moved down to the next point, which isn't being fished.

Tuesday evening

Another super tough day. Stoney bombed and we headed for the north side of Ottertail. It looked like Catfish Creek all over again. Amazing. We pulled in to the next point north, which extended about a quarter of a mile out into the lake before breaking off into 24 feet. I caught a 15-incher right away on a jigging spoon, which brought five boats in around me; something I didn't really appreciate. We continued to work the break and kept catching northerns, but no walleyes. Ottertail was bombing out, as boat after boat came and joined us. It got pretty funny. There were very few fish being caught around us, but boats beget boats and by noon there were 30 boats fishing from the point on in. It was like being on a merry-go-round

Waiting to weigh. The PWT is well organized and the weigh-ins go smoothly, but when you don't have much to show for a hard day's work, the wait can seem like an eternity.

as guys slow-trolled bottom bouncers and spinners or slowly worked live bait rigs. I'm in first flight tomorrow and will come straight there for an hour, then I'm going to get out of this mess. One thing about it, though, we sure didn't get lonely.

There was a major flip-flop at the weigh-in with 51 zeroes and a lot of boats with one fish like me. Gary Roach had three pounds, but only dropped to third. Dan Stier moved into first with a solid limit. He's a real good fisherman and could easily win this event. I think he's one of only three guys fishing Walker Bay. That would explain the bigger fish.

Wednesday, June 4th

I really felt sorry for my day three partner who was Richard Roski from nearby Remer, Minnesota. He fishes the lake all the

One small fish isn't going to help much in this tournament, but every little bit counts towards making the championship.

time and was tearing his hair out as we motored past good spot after good spot that he knew about. But rules are rules, and we both knew that he couldn't tell me. We started at the point north of Ottertail, but caught no fish and left after an hour, hitting all the spots where I caught fish in practice. We caught one nice fish while jigging in the weeds, but that bite died as the lake continued to be pancake flat. Finally, at about one o'clock, we motored back to the point north of Ottertail. Half the tournament field was there, so I know that some fish were being caught. A couple of thunderstorms rolled through during the day, which picked up the wind and the bite. We missed it, but decided to work several hundred yards outside of the boat pack, hoping that some fish moved deeper due to the boat pressure, which often happens.

Dale Dykes came past us, speed trolling bottom bouncers and spinners. He was the only one out as deep as we were. He was smiling and gave me a "thumbs-up" sign, so he must have had some

A massive thunderstorm smashed its way through Walker Minnesota just as the weigh-in was beginning. Several anglers made a terrifying ride in during the storm which nearly destroyed PWT headquarters. Some anglers experienced a hot bite for a few moments immediately preceeding the storm.

fish. The sky was getting pretty dark in the west, so we decided to head in and fish a couple of spots close to the weigh-in site. We just started fishing when the wind picked up and the lightning, rain and hail hit. Being close to a marina, we beached the boat and took shelter there. I don't believe I've ever seen it rain that hard, except maybe during the monsoon season in Korea.

Lightning hit the power pole above the marina, knocking it over, and the wind was snapping off aspen trees like toothpicks. Time was running out, and I really wanted to weigh that one fish, so when the eye of the storm came, we headed for the beach to find the boat half full of water. I turned on the bilge and we pushed and grunted until I could back it out, then plowed our way back to the weigh-in site. Both the first and second flight were already there and there were some pretty scared looks on the faces of some who had come in during the main part of the storm.

Roach was there and he said he caught three fish in five minutes just before the storm hit. "I needed one more minute," he groaned. At the time, he didn't know how prophetic those words would be. My friend and new sporting clays partner, Dale Dykes came from behind and edged him out by one fish. I was really happy for Dale, as this was his first big win, and it couldn't have happened to a nicer guy. Roach took it really well.

Sherry and I took off late after the tournament and got to Garrison, Minnesota on the north shore of Mille Lacs Lake at around 9:00. I was really beat, so we pulled into the Twin Pines Motel and Restaurant and even though it was past serving hours, our host cooked us up a great dinner of roast beef and potatoes and gravy. It was nice to rest and not try to make it home, another six hours away. I discovered that a friend of mine from Wisconsin stays at this resort and my host said that he always complains that there's no big fish in the lake. So for a joke, I gave her a photo of me holding up a 13-pound walleye, and signed it, "to Twin Pines, thanks for the great hospitality and great fishing." We all laughed at his expected reaction to the photo when he comes up this summer.

Thursday, June 5th
It's a foggy morning on the shores of Mille Lacs Lake and I can't believe I slept until 6:30. We're heading down Hwy. 169, and I notice that my trailer lights are blown, not an uncommon occurrence when towing a boat and pulling it out of ramps. I replace the

fuse and all is well, but they suddenly blow again about 100 miles down the road. Obviously a bare wire somewhere, possibly from all the ice on it at the Super Pro. Since it's now daylight and I have signals and brake lights, I decide to just shut my lights off and fix it when I get home. My truck taillights are also out, and I see that the fuse is blown again. So at the next gas stop I load up on fuses, but they don't blow the rest of the trip.

Mercury Nationals

Friday, June 6th

Sherry's birthday today, and I'm on my way to Lake Winnebago in Fond du Lac for the Mercury Nationals Tournament. I found the bare wire on the trailer and fixed that, so I'm back in business, road-wise. The Mercury Nationals is a 300-boat partners tournament sponsored by Mercury Marine and this is their 20th year. Gary Parsons and I will be emceeing the event, which should be fun, although it's weird to not be fishing in it. With the Leech Lake tournament right next to this one, we both felt that we wouldn't have much time to practise, even though we know the lake pretty well. Tonight is the rules meeting and the tournament begins with a 5:30 takeoff tomorrow morning.

Today I did a TV segment for Discover Wisconsin, and we caught three of the nicest walleyes I've ever caught on Lake Winnebago. Now doesn't that just figure! At least it gave me confidence that I still know how to catch these fish! Now I'm thinking I could have won this tournament if I was fishing it, and that's a good thing to think. It shows I may be down after two PWT events, but I'm not out.

After two qualifiers I'm sitting in 105th place overall but only

13 pounds out of the championship. That's easy to make up with two tournaments to go, especially with a summer bite and bigger fish in both systems. I've been down 30 pounds two other years and made it in, so it's still anybody's ballgame, even for some of the guys who are way below me.

My heart goes out to those guys. I know, emotionally, mentally and physically, this can be a very tough profession. I talked to one guy after the tournament who's been gone 29 straight days and he said he was looking forward to going home and getting back to work. Now I don't know if I would go *that* far, but I do understand what he's saying. I remember a stint a few years back when I was gone five straight weeks. It was brutal.

I've also seen more than one guy sitting in his truck with tears in his eyes after a bad tournament because of what he's invested in time and money to fulfill his dream of becoming a professional angler. It's often tough to handle. It's tough to know that you're capable of catching fish and putting a winning program together in practise only to have it fall apart due to weather, or other guys fishing the same spots and dividing up the fish. And it's especially tough to see guys cash a check who didn't catch a fish in practise, or came in and practised one or two days, but got good information from their buddies or locals. It seems unfair, and in a way, it is, especially when you yourself practised from sunrise to sunset every day, often in the worst of weather. But tournament fishing isn't always about fairness. It's about who catches the biggest weight of fish over three days, and when you're dealing with fish, especially walleyes, anything can happen. That's why you forget about the last tournament and move on. It's the only way to keep from beating yourself up to the point that you quit.

Tougher than having a bad tournament is missing your wife and kids and being away this time of the year, missing your kid's graduation. That only happens once in a lifetime, and it's hard to deal with emotionally not only for the angler, but for his family and it puts a strain on the marriage and relationships with the kids, not to mention the financial strain.

I really feel bad for those guys and try to encourage them, because I've been down that road before. In fact, I'm driving a stretch of it right now being in 105th place overall, but it's easier to take when you're sponsored and it's easier to take when you keep things in balance and in perspective. Men often have problems separating work from their family life, and although fishing is fishing, if you do it for a living, it's still a job.

I've been told, "Sure, that's easy for you to say. You're a full-time pro, you're sponsored and you have past successes and we're just trying to get into this thing and we need to do well in order to get our names out and get sponsors." But I tell them not to get discouraged, because sponsors look at more than your ability to catch fish. After all, sponsors fish too, and they know the ups and downs of fishing. They want a complete package, which means they need you to fish the tournaments and get some exposure there, but more importantly, they need you to promote their products one-on-one to the public. Attitude is everything. Believe me, sponsors check your attitude both when you win and when you don't.

Securing sponsorships is one of the toughest and often most frustrating part of professional fishing. Too many fishermen think that if they simply fish the circuit or win a tournament, they should be

Being a sponsored angler is hard work. But, for those willing to put in the effort, the rewards are excellent. Mike McClelland is another angler that understands well the sponsorship end of fishing.

sponsored. First of all, there's several hundred guys fishing various tournaments and companies can't sponsor them all. Secondly, because the skill level of those anglers is pretty equal, it's really tough to win. This year we've already had two new winners in the first two qualifiers and we usually have two or three every season. And most of these guys have been fishing the PWT all nine years. Right now there are only three guys who've won three times and 10 that have won twice.

Once a deal is struck, stay with your sponsor as long as he fulfills his agreement with you. Don't use a sponsor as a stepping-stone to get a few more bucks from his competitor.

Promotion is the real key. You have to be willing to do television interviews, radio shows, be in print media, take media people fishing, all the while talking to them about you sponsor's products. You have to believe in the your sponsor's products, be able to catch fish on them and use them above other products. Obviously, you must promote those sponsors from the weigh-in stage and around the weigh-in area when talking to the local anglers.

I make it a point of giving away a lot of product to locals. That way they can use them, catch fish on them, and believe me, they'll go out and buy more, as well as demand that the local bait shop carry that line of product. It's just good business, and often that person will write a complimentary letter to your sponsor, which goes a long way towards getting re-sponsored at the end of the year.

You also have to be willing to work outdoor trade shows, boat shows, and fishing shows. You need to show the sponsor that you're willing to work for your sponsorship, not just fish. At these shows you're exposed to all the other manufacturer's reps and they see you working the competitor's booth, while their sponsored pro isn't there. I've gotten sponsored by a couple of companies that saw me at the shows year after year and approached me, instead of me approaching them.

You must never, ever, try to promote your sponsor by cutting down the competition to the customer. You might be insulting his taste in tackle by doing so. Sell your sponsor's product on its own merit, not by trashing the competition. That's tacky and that technique gets you a bad reputation around the industry in a heartbeat.

Your honesty and friendship with the industry will land you bookings to speak at these various shows, as sponsors of the show will request that the show promoter put you on the seminar docket. Now you are able to not only promote your sponsors from the speaker's stage or demonstrate their product at the Hawg Trough, but you can tell the audience where you will be after the seminar and they will descend on the booth and purchase the products you talked about. This really opens the eyes of the rep or owner of the company and makes you much more valuable to him than just wearing a patch on your vest at a tournament.

If I'm going to do a seminar at say, Bass Pro, I contact all of my sponsors to make sure that the products I'm talking about will be available to the customer after the seminar. And believe me, they buy them. This makes the store happy and they're more apt to reorder or maybe even increase their next order, which makes the sponsor happy.

Chatting with Ted Takasaki about upcoming promotional events. A sponsored angler's work is never done. Even during a tournament, an angler must be looking for opportunities to promote his sponsors.

As you can see, fishing is only a part of the complete package. It only opens a window of opportunity to promote sponsor products, but that's just a window. There are many other windows and many doors and the angler has to open those doors and walk through them before going to a sponsor and saying "Here's what I can do for you." You see, that's really what the sponsor wants to hear, not "You should sponsor me because I'm fishing the tournament trail."

I started out getting discounts on products from sponsors, or some free product, then worked hard at doing all of the above for those sponsors. Once you have a great track record with a sponsor, you then can take what you've done for them and show that to another non-competing prospective sponsor. Nothing gets a sponsor's attention more than a guy who is willing to work hard to prove his worth.

Once a deal is struck, stay with your sponsor as long as he fulfills his agreement with you. Don't use a sponsor as a stepping-stone to get a few more bucks from his competitor. I've had most of my current sponsors for 10 years and have only left a sponsor when they didn't honor their end of the bargain. Commitment to a sponsor is important to them and to you. For example: once you have a good relationship going, sponsors will put your endorsement or photo on their packaging. If you leave that sponsor the next year for a competitor, there's going to be a lot of stores with that product on the shelves. Now the original sponsor becomes the competitor and you're now in a position of indirectly promoting both, which really puts your credibility in question. And consumers aren't stupid. They know you went to the other company for more money, and if you tell them it was because they made a better product, what does that say about you promoting the other company the previous year, especially with a product you may have designed? That's why working with the same sponsors is not only a great benefit to you, but also to the sponsor.

Yes, sponsorships are tough. There are a lot of players out there. Add to that all of the tournament circuits that also tap into the same sponsors the angler does, and promotional money for a manufacturer can get pretty tight. There are also other events besides tournaments that these companies sponsor, slicing the pie even thinner.

Today, we are seeing some interest from outside of the fishing industry. Auto makers, restaurant chains, motels, oil companies, soft drink companies and many others are showing interest in sponsoring some of the pro fishermen. That's a good sign, because these companies have much deeper pockets. The downside is that these companies don't yet understand the impact of fishing. It's up to the angler, however, to prove to them this is a huge consumer group. And once some companies start sponsoring anglers, their competition will follow suit. Just look at race car driving sponsors and you get my drift.

I encourage anyone who's had a tough tournament to look at it and say "I've done my best for my sponsors, I prefished hard and fished hard in the tournament, and I learned something that will help me down the road. I've seen guys come in an hour early, load up and go home. This is fishin', man. A big fish can bite in the last seconds of the day. Never give up. Never, never, never. As long as that bait's in the water, you have a chance to catch one. And as long as you have a chance to catch a fish, you have a chance to cash a big fish check or add weight to your yearly total toward the championship.

Sponsorships are tough. There are a lot of players out there. Add to that all of the tournament circuits that also tap into the same sponsors the angler does, and promotional money for a manufacturer can get pretty tight.

Yes, the fish have to cooperate and things have to all come together. But almost every tournament winner will tell you that the tournament they won wasn't when they had the best prefishing. They will tell you it just happened. It isn't very often you go into a tournament with a solid game plan and win it. In fact, in the last 10 years, several guys have won that had no clue what they were going to do on the first day. They went out, discovered that the pattern they had and the spots they had were better than they thought, and put three good days together and won. As all-time leading money winner Perry Good would say: "This game is way more mental than people think. All these guys have the skills, but it's winning the mental game that makes a difference." He's right, and I don't think anyone out there wins the mental game more often than Perry.

From the time I got out of the Army in 1970, which was about the time B.A.S.S. started, I had a dream to become a professional fisherman. Of course, everybody has dreams when they're young and their whole life is still ahead of them. The Bass Anglers Sportsman's Society (B.A.S.S.) was in its infancy at that time, and I was really interested in how those guys could be so consistent fishing competitively and make a living doing it. About the same time, I decided to get married and my wife, Sherry, had four children from a previous marriage. We then had another son a year later and when you have a wife and five children, it's difficult to say to them "I'm packing up and I'm heading south to fish B.A.S.S."

So I put the dream aside for awhile, but it never died. In fact, it grew stronger and stronger as I began to fish some local bass and walleye tournaments in the late 70's and early 80's. I bought a bass boat and began to fish more and more tournaments. Now it was really in my blood. In 1988, I started fishing the Masters Walleye Circuit with Scott Hill from Baraboo, Wisconsin. Scott had fished it for two years and pretty much knew the ropes. In fact, if I hadn't agreed to fish with him on the circuit that season, it's doubtful I would have ever become a full-time pro, or even a part-time pro for that matter.

Scott Hill has a notable place in the education of this angler.

Scott taught me a lot about walleye fishing and tournament fishing in general, and how to catch walleyes from different bodies of water. For most of my life, I had fished walleyes in only a few places, mainly on rivers. I would always read about Lake Mille Lacs and Lake of the Woods in Minnesota; Lake Oahe in South Dakota; Lake Erie, Saginaw Bay, Ft. Peck, Montana and Lake Sakakawea in North Dakota and wonder what it would be like to fish on them someday. These were exotic places to me. Places that I never dared to dream that I might fish someday. As of this writing, I've fished them all many times and will again in the future.

Sometimes people tell me how lucky I am to be a professional fisherman, but I would rather use the word "privileged." In spite of the hard work, the miles of driving, the seemingly endless sportshows and bad tournaments, looking at the big picture, I'm doing something that millions of people wish they were doing. How many people can say that about their job? I have to say that I am grateful and often humbled by the privilege of being a pro fisherman because it's something that I always wanted to do and even though there are times of discouragement and even despair, those things are going to happen in life no matter what you do for a living. That happens in life and you just have to grow beyond it and keep going, never losing sight of the original dream, always remembering the blessings.

Part of being a professional is the attitude, and I believe that Ted Takasaki has the best attitude I've ever seen. I've learned a lot from watching him and how he handles adversity.

Part of being a professional is the attitude, and I believe that Ted Takasaki has the best attitude I've ever seen. I've learned a lot from watching him and how he handles adversity. I've seen too many guys fall into the trap of whining and complaining when the fishing gets tough, the wind blows too hard, the tournament management doesn't run the tournament the way they think it should be run, and so on. I know, because I've heard them and sometimes joined them. Management, especially, takes a beating because every decision they make directly affects somebody one way or the other.

They're not perfect, either, but I know that they try their best to pull off a good tournament. Management has a tough job sometimes, balancing the wants and desires of the angler against the needs of the organization. Often forgotten by the angler is that Jim Kalkofen and Mark Dorn don't work for the fishermen. They work for and get paid by management. Yet, I believe they go out of their way to present the angler's viewpoints to management, sometimes sticking their own necks out when they wouldn't really have to. My hat's off to Jim and Mark, as well as to Ron and Al Lindner for having the vision to grow the sport of walleye fishing beyond the buddy tournament level.

Because of their commitment and media presence, other walleye circuits have popped up and flourished. The original walleye circuit, the MWC, boasts full fields at every tournament. I believe that the PWT and the professional image it expresses to the public, has elevated all walleye fishermen to a new level.

Because of walleye tournaments, walleye catch and release, something unheard of a few years ago, is catching on with the general public. Because of walleye tournaments, better boats are being built to handle the rough water with better livewells and recirculators to keep the fish alive. That benefits everyone. Money donated by the pros and various circuits to conservation efforts on the lakes we fish, helps to raise awareness to specific lake management, habitat and stocking needs. Finally, the money spent by tournament anglers during the event and in subsequent trips down the road, is a real boost to the local economy. Also, the knowledge they leave behind helps local anglers to catch more fish!

If an angler is going to call himself a professional, he needs to make every effort to act like one both on and off the water. Sure, we're not perfect and when something gets our goat, it's easy to get a bad attitude. But the constant whining and complaining will be seen not only by the public, but also by the sponsors. And I can tell you, that sponsors want nothing to do with a complainer. Neither does management. There are some issues Jim and Mark and I disagree on, but we've agreed to disagree and move on. That's the best way to handle any impasse, and as Mark Dorn once told me, "If you worry about those kinds of things instead of fishing, it's going to affect the way you fish." You know, he's right. And that goes for other kinds of work as well.

Probably the most complaints come from scheduling, because

some guys fish two or even three circuits, as well as other events. This is tough for management because our window of opportunity to fish in the north is from mid-April to October, and since a lot of guys hunt, they don't like tournaments scheduled in October. I can see the day coming, though, when the schedule will have to be strung out into these border months, especially if the PWT expands, which I believe is going to happen.

Even though a tournament is only three days, we have two days of travel and five days of practise. That's 10 days and sometimes we will have three tournaments a month. In the future, I can see that the pros are going to have to decide to fish one circuit and a couple of invitationals. Some already know that and it's not sitting well with them, but that's just the nature of this business. I expect it to get more competitive with out-of-industry sponsors coming in as well. This is the ninth year of the PWT and it has really taken off. I don't see it being knocked off by a competitor circuit any time soon.

You don't become a fisherman on the professional level, or any level for that matter, without a deep love for the sport. Both my father and grandfather gave me a love for fishing. My dad, Alan Christensen, was born and raised in the city of Kenosha, Wisconsin, but his dad brought him up to Montello fishing whenever he could. Once there, he met my mom, whom he says netted his fish for him. Now that's what I call a prospective wife! They married not long afterward and moved to Montello on the banks of the Fox River and still live there today.

My mother's father, Jack Wheaton, owned a bait shop just below the dam on the Fox, and when I wasn't down there selling him worms or bailing out boats, I was with my dad, catching big bluegills and other fish. My dad loved to catch walleyes on his flyrod and homemade streamer flies (he still does) and both he and my grandpa taught me a lot about river walleyes.

Walleye fishing in this part of the country where the Fox and Wolf Rivers join to form Lake Winnebago and the up river lakes is not only a tradition, but a heritage. And walleye fishing today is as good as it was 100 years ago, thanks to the DNR, Walleyes for Tomorrow and other groups and individuals that have worked hard to maintain this excellent fishery.

Saturday morning, June 7th

It took about an hour to get all the boats launched, which isn't bad considering it was raining pretty hard and quite foggy, and the field numbered 275. With weather like this, I'm kind of glad I'm not out there fishing. Actually, I was supposed to fish with the governor today, but he cancelled out. Must have looked out the window.

Weigh-in started at 2:00 o'clock and lasted it seems, forever, as almost everyone had a limit of fish. What a testimony to this fishery. Another reason it lasted so long is that I knew so many of the fishermen, as did Gary Parsons, and we enjoyed bantering with them. I think it's important that you let everyone cross the stage and have his day in the sun, and allow them to say a few words if they so desire. As a tournament angler, I've been insulted more than once by an emcee who just didn't think it was all that important to let an angler who had a bad day say a few nice things to the crowd. They all paid the same money and fished hard. It's the least an emcee can do for them, even if it means a longer weigh-in.

The catch was so good both days that I'm definitely going to fish this tournament with one of my sons next year. I've never fished a tourney with my two oldest boys, so now's a good time to put it on the schedule.

Thursday, June 12th

I just spent a wonderful day of fishing on Lake Winnebago with Pastor and wildlife artist, Sam Timm and pastor Mark Shaklee who just moved to the area to become youth director at Wautoma Assembly of God. I had never fished with either of them before and they were impressed as we boated three limits of walleyes in about a half day. Now I gotta ask ya: where are those fish when it really counts?

Eastern Pro/Am
Lake St. Clair, Michigan

Friday, June 20th

It's five in the morning and Sherry and I are on I-94 heading for Lake St. Clair, the third stop on the 1997 PWT tour. I anticipate about a nine hour drive, but it's through Chicago and Detroit, so it could be longer. I never look forward to towing a boat through these cities.

Friday evening

We arrived in New Baltimore, Michigan at four o'clock, a total of eleven hours to drive the 500 miles. Needless to say, it was a long and tedious journey. There were accidents everywhere on the interstate and a major accident in Detroit, backing up traffic for miles. My truck began to overheat because temperatures were in the 90's, so I had to turn off the air conditioning. I want you to know it was good to get out of the truck and into an air-conditioned motel.

After a quick, half-hour revival nap, I took a drive down to where the PWT stage was set up and to the bait shop to get a license. It's so hot that I decided to wait on getting bait until morning. Lake St. Clair is located between Lake Huron and Lake Erie and has relatively clear water flowing through it. We can fish the St. Clair River which flows into the lake, the lake itself, and part of the Detroit River which flows out of the lake and on into Lake Erie. Part of both rivers and the lake is in Canada, which is off-limits for the tournament.

Hardly anyone in the tournament has ever fished here before, which should make for an interesting event. I usually like a tournament on new water, because there isn't always a whole lot of information available to incoming fishermen. Most of the locals troll the main lake or handline heavy jigs and rigs in the rivers. There are also big weed beds that should be holding bunches of fish, but these are likely to be small walleyes. I'm going to start in the weeds and work them for a few days before checking out the St. Clair River just before the tournament. With new water and no old spots, prefishing should be quite a challenge.

Saturday, June 21st

Prefishing today was tough, and I have to say that I'm pretty disappointed in the weed bite. Of course the weed beds are thick and massive, with almost the whole lake rimmed with weeds. I can see that it's going to take a lot more than five days to learn the weed bite. There were guys catching some small fish drifting and slow-trolling spinners and crawlers over the tops of deeper weeds in one part of the lake. I didn't try that, but the spot should be easy to find tomorrow: there'll probably be 30 to 50 boats on it.

I had to pull off the water at 1:30 today to drive down to the IX Center in south Detroit to do a seminar for 60 Lakes Marine. The traffic was horrible and it took us two hours to drive the 50 miles. Right now it's 10:30 p.m. and I just got back to the motel incredibly exhausted. I have to do the same thing again tomorrow, but they're predicting temperatures around 100 by noon, so I'm going to try to get to the launch early and get at least six or seven hours in before heading back down to the IX Center.

Sunday, June 22nd

It's only six in the morning and I think everyone else had the same idea. The parking lot and ramp are jammed with boats from jet skis to 28-footers. The best news of the day is that Sherry talked the motel manager into putting one of those little refrigerators in our room, then went out and bought a bunch of crawlers so I wouldn't have to make an extra trip to the bait store every morning. It's really nice to have her along.

The wind is really roaring out of the south today, which is going to make it tough to fish the weeds. I think I'll head south to where the guys were catching some small fish yesterday and try to troll some crankbaits outside of the weed beds, along the edge and perhaps over the top using Wille Sideliner planer boards. That way, I can fish and watch around me to see if very many fish are being taken.

Sunday evening

My plan worked well, and I discovered that northern pike, sheepshead and big rock bass like crankbaits here, just like they do everywhere else. I was right, there were about 50 boats fishing yesterday's hotspot, but very few walleyes were caught. I would have really liked to have been able to pick apart those weeds with jigs, but the wind was blowing too hard for that type of presentation. Drifting spinners and crawlers with the wind seemed to be the order of the day.

Since I already knew the pattern and location, I decided not to take the time to try it, but to keep trolling with the wind, making several passes until 12:00. It was interesting trying to troll with the wind and the boat wakes from what had to be several thousand pleasure boats going in as many directions, all over the lake. Some of these boats are huge! I'm glad tomorrow is Monday and a work day, so the boat traffic shouldn't be too bad.

The traffic to downtown wasn't as bad as yesterday and I think I know why: they were all out on the lake! The seminar went well and the kids that were there really enjoyed it. I was dead dog tired by the time I returned to the motel at 11:30 tonight. But I met a man at the show, who is fishing the tournament as an amateur, and he's going to be fishing with me tomorrow. I've pretty much written off the weed bite. The

It was interesting trying to troll with the wind and the boat wakes from what had to be several thousand pleasure boats going in as many directions, all over the lake. Some of these boats are huge! I'm glad tomorrow is Monday and a work day, so the boat traffic shouldn't be too bad.

fish are too small, there's too many guys already on it, and boat control is a nightmare if there's any wind or boat traffic. So it's off to the St. Clair River tomorrow. I love river fishing, so I'm going to enjoy the day whether I catch any fish or not.

Monday, June 23rd

Well, I finally caught some fish. One weighed 3 1/2 pounds and the other was about 16 inches. There's a good bite going on in a couple of spots on the river, primarily on jigs, bottom bouncers and spinners and locals hand-lining. I saw some really nice fish caught by locals, but they said the bite pretty much dies by 7:00 o'clock in the morning. Great. The earliest I can get there is about 8:00, since the spots are 40 miles from the takeoff and there are two long no-wake zones to go through.

Actually, the fish we caught today were caught in the afternoon out in water quite a bit deeper than what the locals were fishing and I'm wondering if the bite doesn't shut off at all, the fish just move out of where the boats are fishing into deeper water. I'll check that out tomorrow. I know the fish are bigger here from what I saw to-day. I talked with Tom Bruno and he had a 10-pounder caught from the same stretch that I was fishing and he also had a couple of other fish as well. The locals are taking fish in the 5- to 6-pound class, which would blow away this tournament. I've found the right spot, now I have to put the right presentation together and figure out how to catch these fish in the daytime.

Tuesday, June 24th

Boy, do I hate towing a boat through all this traffic! I'm already running later than I thought and I've got that one hour boat ride back up to the river. I'm both physically and mentally exhausted and it's only Tuesday. If I had any sense at all, I'd stay in tomorrow and catch up on my sleep. But I don't have that luxury unless I really put it together today. Naw, I'd feel too guilty. But I am planning to fish the lake tomorrow because I keep hearing about all the fish being caught out there, although they are running small. I did talk to one guy, however, who said he and his buddies went to the lake to catch some of those "eaters" and all they could catch were 8-pounders. Now there are stories like this at every tournament, and, of course, he couldn't remember where he was fishing, but he assured me it was true. I thought this would be a good story to pass on to a few of the rumor-mongers, drawing them away from the river bite. There's no wind today, so I assume the lake is going to get fished pretty hard. I hope to put in nine hours on the river today and get back at a decent hour and get a good night's sleep.

Tuesday evening

It's 7:00 p.m. and I'm heading back north on I-94 right behind some big ol' semi, trying to make it back in time to pick up some bait before the store closes. I ended up fishing until 6:00 because I caught five fish today, four that measured. They were only 16-inchers, but three came off of one little rock pile in the river, and all three were caught vertical jigging a half-ounce Mann-O-Lure spoon. I'm hoping that the spot will produce early in the day, since I didn't really fish it until afternoon.

I wish those fish would have been bigger, but they're the same size fish that the guys are catching in the lake. The only difference is that they appear to be fatter from the river, so there's a little extra weight there, plus there are some bigger fish around. Instead of going to the lake tomorrow, like I planned, I'm going back up to the

The rigging of rods and preparing of boat and equipment are jobs that never seem to end.

river and cover more water pulling bottom bouncers and spinners against the current in deeper water. I have a hunch those bigger fish are out there, maybe as deep as 40 or more feet.

Wednesday, June 25th

The wind blew 40 mph today, which means that there were a lot more boats in the river than there would or should have been for the last practise day. There were guys up there fishing all over, but most of them were just running up and down the river looking to see where everyone was fishing. As a result, I stayed away from where I caught fish the past two days and worked a favorite local spot, a power plant discharge where there were maybe four other boats. Right in front of them all I whacked a 5-pounder, which wasn't too cool. Even though I tried to hide the fish, it was hooked so well that it just came to the top and started splashing. The other guys all saw it, so I just pulled it in, unhooked it and released it. Fortunately, by the time they saw the fish, I had drifted about 200 yards from where it first bit, so they weren't real sure where I actually caught it. The fish came on a bouncer and spinner and I saw another good fish caught on the same combo in the same area. I'm going to start at the plant tomorrow, then work some of my other spots where I caught fish later in the day.

Thursday, June 26th, Day One of the Eastern Pro-AM

My day one partner is Craig Jackel from Austin, Minnesota. I know Craig and I know he is an excellent fisherman. In fact, he's one of those guys who could turn pro anytime he wanted to. I hope, that with a good stick in the boat, we'll be able to take a limit of fish and have a couple of bigger fish to go with them.

Thursday evening, Day One

The plan worked great, only we didn't get the limit we were looking for. Takeoff was at 7:00 a.m., but we didn't get up to the power plant until 8:20 because it was farther up the river than I had been fishing all week and I decided to take a "shortcut" that I hadn't taken before and got into the wrong channel. That loss of time might have really hurt us, and was a stupid thing to do on my part, especially knowing about that early morning window the fish were biting on.

I caught a 2 1/4-pounder on the first pass and Craig whacked a

5.88 about an hour later. A possible limit looked good, but that was our only two fish of the day. At 1:00 o'clock we began to work our way back down river, hitting some of the spots where I caught smaller fish during the week. If only we could have gotten on one tiny school! As it turned out, Craig won the big fish award for the day, worth $675 which we split, and our two fish weighed 8.23 pounds, which is currently 33rd place. Seventeen pounds is leading, which means I need to take at least three or four good fish a day to get back in it.

I'm in the last flight, so tomorrow is my short day, which is going to really make it tough, losing all that fishing time by running up the river. I could go to the lake, but the fish are small and the bite isn't all that great out there. Besides, four of the top five guys are fishing the river, so I know the fish are bigger where I am. I just need to work harder and try to put more of those bigger fish in the boat.

Friday, June 27th, Day Two
My partner today was Herb Franks, the same guy I drew at

Craig Jackel's 5.88-pounder was a big help to our day-one weight. It also won us $675 in big-fish money.

Dubuque. We made the long run and started the day off with a bang by catching two big fish, one 5 1/2-pounder and one almost six pounds. Herb caught one of them vertical jigging, while I caught one on a spinner. We then lost another big fish, which really made both of us sick. Four more of these, and I'm leading the tournament. Unfortunately, we could only add a 16-incher the rest of the day. Since we had to be back by 3:15, we had to pull out at 2:15, making for a really short day. With the waves from the big boats pounding us all the way across the lake, we barely made it in on time.

Our weight for the day was 12.60 which pushed me into 17th place and 13 pounds out of first. If I could catch six of those big fish tomorrow, I could win this tournament. But that's an awful big IF! It's decision time. The bite got really good in the lake and guys told me I could catch a limit of those small fish pretty easy, and that would probably keep me in the money. On the other hand, how often is a guy in a possible position to win a tournament? I know the fish are bigger in the river. Catching six of them would be a real long shot, but possible. I also know that most of the field will be out

Weighing three nice fish on day two bolted me to 17th place.

in the lake, since the bite picked up, and that I would pretty much have the best spots in the river to myself. When there's a choice between going for the win or just cashing a check, there's no question: you go for the win.

The other factor is qualifying weight for the championship. With my current weight, I'm only six pounds out of it, so even if I have a so-so day in the river, I should be able to maintain that. Sherry and I agreed to go for it, so that's tomorrow's plan. Besides, I have a good partner in Hans Schneeberger from Oregon, Wisconsin tomorrow, and that should help. I hope.

Saturday, June 28th, Day Three

When it's meant to be, it happens, but today it wasn't meant to be. Hans and I worked really hard, but managed only three small fish. At noon, we toyed with heading out to the lake and trying to catch three more for a limit and a good check. But I didn't come here to cash a check, I came to win, so we stuck it out the rest of the day in the river. It was a disappointing finish—I dropped all the way to 36th place and out of the money—in a tournament in which I could have done really well, but there's no time to think about it. Fort Peck is coming up in a week and it's going to take that long to get physically and mentally ready.

Sunday, June 29th

We decided to sleep over and take off early this morning. Instead of driving through Chicago, we opted for the northern route through the Upper Peninsula, even though it would take us a couple of extra hours. The route is beautiful, crossing the Mackinac Bridge between lake Michigan and Lake Huron, then driving along over 150 miles of Lake Michigan shoreline.

The bite got really good in the lake and guys told me I could catch a limit of those small fish pretty easy, and that would probably keep me in the money. On the other hand, how often is a guy in a possible position to win a tournament?

We took our time, reflecting on Lake St. Clair and thinking about Ft. Peck, hoping to put on a good show there and make it into the championship. We have a few days to get ready for that, which is good. I'm so worn out that it's going to take me a week to get fired up for Peck. But I WILL be fired up!

Western Pro/Am
Fort Peck Reservoir
Glasgow, Montana

Monday, July 7th

Sherry's busy packing clothes and gathering "travel food" for our trip to Ft. Peck, Montana and the Western Pro-AM. I went down to Madison today to Bait Rigs Tackle and got resupplied with bottom bouncers and spinners and components as well as about two pounds of jigs. St. Clair had a lot of snags and we lost all the rigs I had put together after Ouachita. I also stopped at Gander Mountain to pick up a few things there, and ended up spending half the day there talking to customers about jigs, spoons and crankbaits. I didn't get back until late afternoon and there's this huge pile of stuff to pack into the Suburban for the 1,000 mile trip. Our plan is to leave at about 4:00 a.m. and at least make it to Bismarck, North Dakota by nightfall. Then we'd only have about an eight-hour drive the next day.

I'll be doing a fishing seminar on Wednesday for the anglers fishing in the Montana Governor's Cup which is this weekend. It will be held at the Cottonwood Inn, where we're staying, so I should be there in plenty of time for that. My 11-year old Suburban is running okay, and just turned over to 160,000 miles. The third transmission only has about 10,000 on it, but the engine is original. It's starting to burn a little oil and leak a little antifreeze, and tends to overheat if driven over 65 mph, so I just have to baby it a little. The weather forecast is chilly for the 7th of July, with last night's record low of 39 degrees. But that makes the old truck run cooler, and I like that.

I've never been a real hot weather person, but I don't care for extreme cold either. I like Wisconsin's four seasons, however, it's just that spring and fall are way too short and the six months of winter is just too darn long. Summer temperatures topping off around 80 would be perfect and winter temperatures topping at 32 would be great. Does anyone know of a state that has that kind of weather?

The forecast is for lots of rain here the next few days, which will be really good for the new trees I planted. This will be a 13-day trip, and my plants and lawn either grow fast or die during these trips. Fortunately, our neighbors and friends, Bill and Bonnie Brooks, check the place and water the plants. It's nice to have good neighbors like them.

Tuesday, July 8th

We made it all the way to Dickinson, North Dakota, just east of the Montana border. We are going to take a two hour side trip through Theodore Roosevelt National Park early in the morning, then keep going on to Ft. Peck. About half way out here, I noticed the boat bouncing a little on the trailer. Somehow the winch catch broke, so I'm going to have to get a new one when I get to Ft. Peck.

Wednesday, July 9th

We're on the road again and swung into McDonald's for an on-the-road breakfast. It's probably going to take a little longer to get to Ft. Peck, since the temperature is supposed to crack 100 today, and that means driving slower. We just came out of the park, and it was beautiful, with lots of free ranging bison, and more importantly, no people this early in the morning.

Wednesday evening

Fort Peck Reservoir looked a lot different when we crossed the five-mile long dam this afternoon. I was here last fall doing a photo shoot for In-Fisherman and the water was at least eight feet lower than it is right now. I already have a game plan in place, and I'll be fishing just outside the border with Jim Kalkofen tomorrow.

Prefishing actually starts on Saturday, but we can fish outside of the tournament boundary and I figure it will take me a day to catch up on getting everything rigged, the winch fixed, and my body rested before official practise begins.

Jim arrived last night and discovered this morning that someone had cut the straps on his boat cover and had broken into his truck, stealing at least $3,000 worth of equipment. That's something you don't expect to happen out in this part of the country. I think I'm going to try to find some other place to keep my rig for the week, even though the hotel has promised to beef up security.

The theft didn't seem to dampen Jim's enthusiasm for Ft. Peck, however, as we had a good time doing a co-seminar tonight for the Governor's Cup contestants. We'll be fishing tomorrow and hopefully catch a few fish to put some kind of a pattern together early in the game. We'll have to make a three-hour drive to the tournament boundary, since it's against tournament regulations to go there by boat. This is wild country out here, and the nearest ramp for us is way past the western border. After the three hour truck trip, we'll have another hour-long boat ride to get to the border.

Thursday, July 10th

We really had a fun day of fishing today, catching many walleyes and probably averaging four pounds. Most of the fish were caught within a mile of the border, so I expect the bite to be pretty much the same inside the border and am going to find that out on Saturday or Sunday. Jim's son, Nate, fished with us and we all caught several fish casting jigs and half crawlers to points and rocky shoreline breaks. I caught three on jigging spoons and will be looking at fine-tuning that pattern a little closer to the take off. We marked both the north and south ends of the western border and found we were 47 miles from the takeoff as the crow flies. Probably more like 50-52 by water. That could be a long run in rough water, but I might have to do it if I can't find a good bite to the east.

Friday, July 11th

The first day of the Governor's Cup is over and the first place team had 25 pounds for five fish, which is an excellent weight. Since they can only run about 10 miles west, it tells me that there are some pretty good fish close. Big fish for the day was 11 pounds, 12 ounces. That's a hawg! Their second day is tomorrow, which is our first day of practise. My plan is to get out early and get outside of their boundary so I'm not catching any of their fish while their tournament is going on. I'll probably run up the Dry Arm where I caught some big fish last fall. The water's clearer up there and it might be a good jigging spoon bite. Hardly anyone fishes this stretch in the summer, but I might as well give it a try and get it out of my system.

Saturday, July 12th

It's 4:30 a.m. and I'm hooking up the boat, hoping to get on the water before the long lines of the Governor's Cup folks begin to form. Dan and Mary Humbert, who live about five miles from the Cottonwood Motel, have graciously allowed me to park my boat at their house. I know it will be safe there, and I don't have to hunt for a plug-in every night when I get off the water. Since I plan to fish long days, my four batteries are going to take a beating. Dan has offered his extra charger, so I can charge all four at the same time. That's going to really help as the week goes on.

Friday evening

The first day of practise is over and it sure was a long day. I fished my first spot at 5:00 a.m. and loaded the boat on the trailer at 7:00 p.m. I only caught one small walleye in the Dry Arm, so that area of the lake is definitely out of my system.

It took 38 pounds to win the Governor's Cup, with the winners not having any fish larger than five pounds. That tells me that it's not going to take 75-90 pounds to win the PWT tournament, as predicted, but probably more like 60. My guess right now is that the bite is better farther west, with bigger fish and more of them. I'll know after tomorrow, because that's where I'll be fishing.

Sunday, July 13th

I love it when a plan comes together. The "plan" was to run to the border and fish my way back, but I never got more than 26 miles from the dock. I started fishing sharp-breaking shorelines from Bell Point to the west and caught some great fish off of just about every spot. The ticket was to hold the boat out in 20 feet and cast a half-ounce Hopkins spoon into about five feet of water then snap-jig it down the drop. They really hammered it. I also went back through the same areas with a 1/8-ounce Odd'Ball Jig and crawlers and caught several more, so I know that I have the right technique.

My total weight for the day would have been at least 30 pounds for my best six fish. Of course, I had a 10-pounder in the mix, but my other fish averaged a solid four pounds. Even without the big fish, I know that three days of this kind of weight will win it easily. Right now, I'm not sure if I even need to make the border run. Still, I better at least spend one day up there in case there's a mega-bite going on.

Monday, July 14th

Got a little lazy today, not launching the boat until 7:00 a.m. That good day yesterday has given me a lot of confidence about this tournament and the pattern I'm fishing. In fact, I slept really well last night, for the first time in months. Now, instead of fishing simply to qualify for the championship, I'm looking at a chance to win. It was close to 100 degrees today for the third straight day, and even though I've been in the sun and on the water all year, my face and arms are pretty blistered.

It was another productive day. I decided to pull bottom bouncers and spinners in the same areas I caught the fish yesterday, and caught a lot of fish, but all small. I talked to a few other spinner fishermen who said their fish were running small as well. I then went back through the areas with jigs and spoons, and caught a few bigger fish on them. There seems to be a good number of fish holding on these points right now. I hope that doesn't change by tournament time.

My total weight for the day would have been at least 30 pounds for my best six fish. Of course, I had a 10-pounder in the mix, but my other fish averaged a solid four pounds. Even without the big fish, I know that three days of this kind of weight will win it easily.

Tuesday, July 15th

It's 5 a.m. and Craig Jackel, who I fished with in the Lake St. Clair tournament, is waiting for me at the dock. Since this is my last long day of prefishing, I might make the long run to the border. Craig is willing to fish until dark, so I've got 36 gallons of gas in the boat and a lot of bait for the day. It's supposed to be in the high 90's again today and calm winds. I heard there were some fish going in the Snow Creek area, about 15 miles from the border. We're going to have to check that out today.

Tuesday evening

It's 10 p.m. and I just got the boat gassed up and the chargers on it and I'm heading back to the motel. The day was a long one and I'm totally exhausted. We made it up to the border and caught a few fish up there, but not what I expected. Snow Creek also produced a few nice fish, but nothing like what I was catching further east. We did catch a lot of fish today, and our best six would have weighed around 22 pounds, again, with a 10-pounder thrown in. Take away that fish, and we're looking at 14 pounds or so. That's not going to be enough. We put on over 100 miles and probably fished 50 different points today. I wasn't impressed. Unless a miracle occurs tomorrow, I'm planning to stay within 30 miles of the takeoff and simply fish as many points as I can to put a limit of 3- to 4-pound fish in the boat.

I'll be fishing with Bernie Barringer and Mary Humbert tomorrow. My plan is to fish close, within 10 miles of the takeoff and get

Points like this one were loaded with 3- and 4-pound walleyes. In only a couple hours jigs and jigging spoons would easily catch a limit.

off the water by one o'clock. With three people in the boat tomorrow, I can try a couple of different things. I'm almost afraid to fish close. I did that in 1991 out here, fishing close the last day of practise and catching lots of nice fish, which completely changed my game plan. Those fish never did go during the tournament.

Wednesday, July 16th

Bernie and I picked up the boat and Mary at her house and got on the water at 6:00 a.m. It was another hot, sticky day in the mid-90's, but we boated a limit of fish by nine o'clock that would have weighed over 20 pounds. We continued to catch fish the rest of the morning, and never went more than six miles from the weigh-in. I was afraid this would happen. Now I had to make a decision whether to make the 30-mile run tomorrow, or fish all these close spots. I believe that there's a good number of fish on these new spots, and only a handful of guys fishing them. On the other hand, most of the 120 boat field is west and fishing the same areas I was the past four

Pairings are announced at the rules meeting the evening before the tournament. Eppie Esquibel of Rawlins, Wyoming will be my day-one partner.

days. I'll check the weather and make my decision in the morning.

Thursday, July 17th, Day one of the Western Pro-Am

It's day one and wouldn't you know it: after five calm days of practise, the wind is howling out of the southeast at 20-25 mph. My partner today is Eppie Esquibel from Rawlins, Wyoming. I don't know who's more nervous, me or him. He's really looking forward to the day and learning more about walleye fishing. I hope he isn't disappointed. The wind is supposed to build all day, although it's dying down somewhat right now. I've made the decision to fish those close spots first, then move west about nine o'clock, unless I have a limit by then.

Thursday evening

In 20 years of tournament fishing I've had plenty of frustrating days, but today had to be the worst. I cut across the reservoir to my first spot and Steve Poll was there netting a nice fish. I waved and went around to the next spot and Ted Takasaki was there netting a fish. I waved to him, too, then went to my third spot where I made a cast with a spoon, hooked a good fish and it got off. I then went to my fourth point and the same thing happened. The rest of the day didn't get any better. The winds did build as predicted, 30-40 mph, gusting to 50 at weigh-in time. Many of the guys who went a long distance didn't make it back in time. When you're late, you lose all your weight for the day. It cost a half dozen guys a chance at qualifying for the championship.

We ended up catching only two fish for a little over two pounds. I was six miles from the weigh-in and it took me 25 minutes to get in. The waves were pretty big. Both Steve Poll and Ted Takasaki weighed a limit of fish. Steve said when I saw him, he was netting his third fish. He encouraged me to fish the same area again tomorrow, but I don't know. Even though I prefished those spots, I don't want to spoil Steve or Ted's chance at winning the tournament. Both of them are pulling spinners around the points. Steve is working each point back and forth, but Ted is simply covering a lot of water from point to point, picking up scattered fish.

Quite often when a big blow comes in, the fish will do a couple of things. Some will congregate on main points, like the one Steve was fishing. Others will scatter all over the place and Ted picked up on that. I could pull spinners tomorrow and cover more water, and still fire a few casts with jigs or spoons into the shallows and tips of the points. I've done that before and have done well, so that's my strategy for tomorrow. Hopefully the wind will die and I'll be able to fish further west. It's my long day tomorrow, so my plan is to hit those close spots, then head west.

Friday, July 18th, Day two

My partner today is Myron Sylte from Williston, North Dakota and both of us agree that it's going to be a tough day. Winds 60-70 mph blew through last night, along with a couple of tornados. Everything is blown down at the weigh-in stage and the ramp and parking lot are a muddy mess. The wind is northwest at 15 mph and is supposed to remain there all day. One thing's for sure, we won't be sweating today!

Stepping down off the stage after day one, that look tells the story. Unbelieveable.

Friday Evening

Fishing was tough all over today, but some guys way to the west did well. We didn't. It was another frustrating day as we caught one fish in the first spot, then lots of small fish the rest of the day with no keepers. I did manage to fish as many spots as possible, but with the bite getting tougher in this cold front, nothing seemed to work. I tried to keep my attitude upbeat, but it was tough. By the end of the day, I had pretty much resigned myself to the fact that I wouldn't be at the Championship. Well, there's still tomorrow and the big fish pools as well as the Pinnacle Award for breaking the current PWT big fish, which is 12.12 pounds. I'm reminded of the 13-pounder I caught here last fall and I'm beginning to get encouraged.

Matt Jacobson nearly missed the Pinnacle $25,000 bounty. His 11.34-pounder was only 3/4 of a pound too small. Will Lage had the big fish of the tournament, an 11.37-pounder.

Saturday, July 19th, Day three

I'm watching the weigh-in and the day is mercifully over, at least for some of us. The wind blew hard out of the northeast all day and the bite got very, very tough. My partner Steve Harada, from nearby Wolf Point, and I caught a nice sauger right away and that was it. And if that wasn't frustrating enough, my day one partner, Eppie Esquibel, told me his brother caught a limit of 3-pounders casting jigs and leeches from the causeway about two miles from the takeoff site. He was just fishing off the bank for fun! After pondering that for a few moments, some of the disappointment and frustration turned into laughter at the excitement on his brother's face as he retold the story to me and how proud he was about catching those fish!

Today wasn't only frustrating for me, but for about half the field as most of them zeroed or had one or two fish. Perry Good won it, fishing by himself and fishing a strong mental tournament as conditions changed daily. I was in good company, as former winners and longtime championship qualifiers Mike McClelland, Gary Parsons, Steve Fellegy, Keith Kavajecz and many others didn't make the championship. It was a real strange year and I hope it hasn't become a trend. All of these guys pretty much fish alone, away from the boat packs. None made the big show.

I was in good company, as former winners and long-time championship qualifiers Mike McClelland, Gary Parsons, Steve Fellegy, Keith Kavajecz and many others didn't make the championship. It was a real strange year and I hope it hasn't become a trend.

Sunday, July 20th

One thing about a 1,000 mile drive home is that it gives a person a lot of time to think and reflect on the past season. We pulled out of Glasgow at 4:00 a.m. with the intention of driving straight home, resting up for a few days, before leaving on a 10-day missions trip to Healy, Alaska. One of the things that happens after a year like this, is that doubt begins to enter the mind. I don't believe I've ever felt so discouraged about a tournament year, and even my wife, who is usually so upbeat, broke into tears as we talked about this past week. I had never seen this in her before, and it made me want to quit right then and there.

I don't usually stay in a funk for very long and neither does Sherry. By the time we rolled in at 11:00 p.m., we were too tired to care. Besides, tomorrow we would be putting plans together for our trip and we were excited about that. Still, I couldn't help but be a little disturbed at how many of the longtime pros didn't make the championship. And what bothered me more than that, was that some guys made it fishing in boat packs and fishing other people's fish when theirs didn't go. I don't like that scenario and I hope that this year was simply a fluke and that next year things will come back into balance. Keith, Gary and Mike expressed those same concerns as well.

The nature of walleyes is often to concentrate at high levels in certain areas of a river or lake, thus attracting large numbers of fishermen. While I believe that almost every tournament fisherman would like to have a "honey hole" all to himself, far too many of them are willing to forego the extra work of finding that honey hole, opting for the easy spots instead, which creates the boat packs.

Walleye fishing is very popular with local anglers as well, and they often gravitate to boat packs, creating even bigger packs. I've seen schools of boats numbering 400 to 500 and have seen tournament guys do really well fishing these packs. But it doesn't take a rocket scientist to locate these fish, and some pros have gotten awful good at not only locating the packs, but catching qualifying fish in them.

In a few tournaments over the past 10 years, the only school of fish was in the packs. So there are times when the pack has to be fished. The smart guys; however, will move to the outside and fish those fish that have been pressured away from the big boat pack. Some, however, will remain right in the pack, sometimes fishing only a few feet apart, or even bumping boats. I'll tell you what, folks. That's not tournament fishing to me. I've had to fish packs a few times over the years, and I try to find something different on the bottom, or get to the edge, instead of just vertical jigging or pulling spinners through the same area everyone else is fishing. Sometimes it works, sometimes it doesn't, but at least I feel like I'm doing something different.

My aversion to packs is that I came out of bass fishing tournaments, where you wouldn't even fish the same bay as another contestant, let alone the same weed bed or rock pile. But walleyes aren't bass, and sometimes, and I stress *sometimes*, it's necessary to fish the only school of biting fish. But not in every tournament. Some anglers have also grown up in a part of the country where you look for other boats to help you locate fish. I didn't, so when I first saw this, I couldn't believe it. Yet I was surprised that the first boat didn't even get upset with the second boat coming in to fish his spot. So geographical and cultural aspects come into play here as well. One of my greatest fears is that I'm going to win one of these tournaments fishing in a pack and have to face the derision of the packman. But with my philosophy of finding my own fish and fishing my own spots, that's not likely to happen any time in the near future.

The PWT has put boundaries on our tournament waters, and I think, in at least a few cases, this has added to the pack problem. When Gary Parsons made the 250-mile round-trip run at Mobridge a few years ago that won him the tournament and bumped me into second, a lot of guys called for restricting water. I can't say that I

Forty happy anglers going to the PWT championship. Chris Gilman won Angler-of-the-Year.

was happy with the outcome of that day, but I have to give Gary credit for going for the home run. And that tournament has been talked about more than any other over the past 10 years. In fact, folks are still talking about it wherever we go.

On the other hand, it is nice not to have to worry about having enough gas in the boat, and the PWT is concerned about guys getting too far out of radio range (and TV range), so safety comes in to play as well. It's not likely that the PWT will lift tournament boundaries anytime soon. And that's not really the answer to solving the pack fishing problem. I do know this: pack fishing has had very few winners over the past 10 years. It's still the guy who fishes alone, on one or two spots, who usually cashes the first place check. And that reason alone, might possibly cause many of the packmen to begin prefishing with a different philosophy. Let's hope so. After all, shouldn't it be the philosophy of professional tournament fishing to catch fish that no one else is fishing? It's something for all of us to think about anyway.

August 18th

Sherry and I just spent the past 13 days in Alaska and really enjoyed our time. We went with 10 other people from our church and spent most of a week working on a new parsonage for a pastor in the town of Healy. It was a rewarding time and we managed to squeeze in a day to go to Denali Park and see the wildlife there. Before we came back, some of the group went halibut fishing and caught a bunch. I didn't go. I had just as much fun watching the red sockeye salmon in the Ninilchik River. It was just cool watching them jump and swim right along the shoreline. I would have enjoyed catching a couple, though! We got back home on the 17th and I'll be getting ready to fish the MWC tournament on Lake Winnebago with my son, Steve, with prefishing starting on Wednesday.

Masters Walleye Circuit
Lake Winnebago, Wisconsin

Wednesday, August 20th

It's been a month since Ft. Peck and I'm feeling fully recovered from the tournament year. In fact, I'm kind of fired up about competing in the MWC again on Lake Winnebago, in what a lot of anglers are calling a pretty tough tournament. I'll be fishing it with my son, Steve, and will be picking him up this morning at seven o'clock in Oshkosh. Winnebago usually has a pretty good algae bloom this time of year and it makes the fishing kind of tough. I know, however, that the water will be cleaner to the north end of the lake, so we plan to concentrate our efforts there.

Thursday, August 21st

Steve and I had a pretty good day yesterday, catching a limit of fish in a pretty short time, casting 1/8-ounce Odd'Ball jigs tipped with half crawlers over the tops of the shallow reefs. Most of the fish came from two feet of water, which isn't surprising with the water temperature a cool 67 degrees. It should be about 80 degrees this time of year, so it looks like these fish are beginning to move into their fall patterns already.

The lake is real dirty due to lots of strong winds and heavy rain. Even though I'm sure we'll be fishing that area during the tournament, I'm going to check out the up river lakes of Butte des Morts,

Poygan and probably the Wolf River today. Steve has to work this morning, so I'll fish those spots alone, then pick him up and head out into the main lake.

Thursday evening

I hit all the up river areas this morning, but only caught one small fish. The water is really dirty up there with all the runoff and the temperature is continuing to fall, with a high air temperature today in the 50's. That's cool even for Wisconsin in August. I picked up Steve and we spent the last couple hours of the day fishing some other reefs near where we fished yesterday, and caught some nice fish. I think we have the pattern and the spots. We just need to find a few more places in case these bomb, which is a normal occurrence on Lake Winnebago.

Friday, August 22nd

Steve had to work again this morning and he's lucky, because there was a north wind howling down the lake and really whipping up the water. I foolishly decided to check out a spot to the south that had always been a good producer. It took an hour to get there and the water was chocolate milk in color, so I simply turned around and headed back into those lovely five-foot waves. I tried fishing some other spots close to Oshkosh which is where the weigh-in is, but the wind and dirty water just wasn't cutting it. I finally pulled off the water early to get ready for the pre-tournament meeting. I feel good about the north reefs, but they're calling for a change in wind tomorrow and warmer weather, so we'll see how that affects the bite.

Saturday, August 23rd

We took off in the cool of the morning on relatively flat water and were happy to find our first spot unoccupied by other fishermen. We caught a fish right off the bat, but it took us until 11 o'clock to catch our limit of five fish. With four hours of tournament time left, we decided to get out of there and look for some bigger fish. Wisconsin law doesn't allow culling, but state law allows us to catch five fish apiece, so we could still catch five more fish and weigh our best five out of the 10. So we checked out every reef in the area and fished some good river spots, but never boated another walleye. I was kind of surprised and a little disappointed, since I felt confident that we would be able to put a few bigger fish in the boat and maybe weigh 10 or 11 pounds for the day.

As it turned out, the bite was as tough as a lot of guys claimed it was, and our 8.04 pounds put us in 28th place out of 200 boats. Only 12.90 was leading so a few more good fish would have put us right in there. Heavy thunderstorms are predicted for tonight, with sunny skies and light winds for tomorrow. Our strategy will be the same as today: try to get eight pounds in the boat, then work on getting some bigger fish. With a catch of 12-13 pounds, I think we have a legitimate shot at winning it.

Saturday night

I'm walking across the parking lot of the Pioneer Inn at Oshkosh and it's raining so hard I can barely see the door to the lobby. I'm speaking at the Fellowship of Christian Anglers meeting tonight, then heading over to Steve's house for a good night's sleep. This rain is incredible. If it blows through by morning, I'm expecting a mega-tough bite tomorrow.

Sunday, August 24th

Day two is over and it proved to be just what I had expected. Very tough. We got to our spot through the drizzle and fog to find a local guy trolling crankbaits along the edge of the reef. He shook his head as we eased by, indicating he wasn't catching anything, so I hoped the fish were up on top like they were yesterday. We found the shallowest spot, about two feet, and dropped a small marker buoy on it, then cast the area, but no luck. Actually, a school of smallmouth bass had moved on it and we were catching them with regularity. But we needed walleyes.

Finally, at nine o'clock, Steve caught a nice 2-pound fish. Even though I was entertaining thoughts of trying some other reefs, we were catching fish here, smallies and sheepshead, so the walleyes had to be there and just not biting. At 12:30 I'd had enough and was working my way toward the buoy to pick it up when Steve hooked another nice fish, this time off the edge in about five feet of water.

That sealed it. We were staying no matter what. All the while we were fishing the wind began to blow harder and harder out of the northwest, but the reef was fairly close to the west shore, so it was pretty fishable. We had to be in by three o'clock and were running out of time. At 2:30 we had four fish in the livewell and a mini bite was on, but we had to get out of there if we were going to get back in time.

I knew the wind would be much worse around the point, but at least we'd be going with it. We made it back with less than a minute to go, stopping twice to fill the livewell with fresh water. I had underestimated the wind and waves. It's a good thing we left when we did. Our four fish weighed only a little over five and a half pounds, giving us 13.64 for the tournament and a 29th place finish. As predicted, 21 pounds won it.

This tournament was a moral victory for me after the year I was having. We made a check and that was good, but more importantly, I felt good about how we fished against the best anglers on the MWC as well as the best local talent on Lake Winnebago. Tournament director, Bob Kaczkowski gave me over 15 minutes of stage time while they tabulated the results and it gave me a great opportunity to promote my sponsors and to hype the fishing on Lake Winnebago to a big crowd. After that, we did an interview with TV26 that would air on the evening news.

The MWC has one more tournament this year on the Petenwell Flowage, which is about 45 miles from my home. Unfortunately, it's the same weekend as a two-day bass tournament that I was going to fish with my son, Alan. Of course, we could fish the walleye tournament, but I was kind of looking forward to putting away the walleye rods and digging out all my bass stuff. I had fished this tournament for several years and had missed it the last two, so I'm planning to do the bass tournament instead of Petenwell.

Postseason 1997

Thursday, September 18th

I'm out on Lake Puckaway prefishing for the two day bass tournament that's being held this weekend and I'm having a blast. The fish are in two feet of water in small open water pockets in thick weeds. They are also in the reeds and I'm catching them by casting a Mann's Shadow, which is a soft plastic topwater twitch bait, rigged weedless on a new Mustad Needlepoint hook. The fish are really aggressive, but not real easy to get to in the thick weeds. But they sure do dance across the water in these shallows and I doubt that too many guys will be fishing this pattern.

Friday, September 19th

Not wanting to burn my spot I found yesterday, I moved to another weed bed several hundred yards down the lake and caught some fish in there as well. Now we had two spots, and while a few guys were fishing the deeper edges of the weeds, no one went right into them like I did. The weather was calm and beautiful the past two days, but a big cold front is supposed to come in tonight (the weather is no respecter of bass or walleye fishermen) and that might really put these fish off the bite.

Saturday, September 20th

The wind hasn't gotten here yet, but the air is cold, in the 30's and the lake is a solid bank of fog. Visibility is about 30 feet, but the tournament director is sending us out, encouraging us to take it slow. No kidding. Most of the anglers don't have a GPS, but I do and even though our spot is within sight of the takeoff on a clear day, I punched it into my GPS yesterday just in case it was foggy.

We idled to our spot and of course, had it all to ourselves. It looked good in the early darkness with no wind, and we caught two good fish almost immediately. We also lost two really good fish that got down in the thick weeds and pulled off. We could hear a few other boats fishing nearby, especially when they boated a fish, even though we couldn't see them. About two hours later the fog lifted, or should I say the fog blew out with a 30 mph northwest wind. It took the bite with it.

Sunday, September 21st

Our two fish yesterday kept us in the hunt for the money, but possibly even the win, in spite of one team bringing a limit of 10 fish to the dock. Anything can happen in a two-day bass tournament and if we can catch a limit today, and they bomb, we still have a chance. The air temperature is below freezing and the wind is still blowing out of the northwest at about 20 mph. A couple of teams that zeroed yesterday have already called it quits.

With this cold front, I need to go with a smaller bait and fish it slower, something I should have done yesterday when the bite went off. I know for sure that the second place team was fishing small stuff and they had eight fish. I also know that the first place team probably won't change tactics from yesterday, so there's a good chance to sneak up on them.

Sunday afternoon

The first day leaders pulled out the win, catching one fish 10 minutes before check-in. We were talking to them as they caught it, fishing about 30 yards from us. We only had two fish again today, and the bite was simply horrible, as was the wind. It never did get above 45 degrees, so the chill factor never got above freezing. Our two fish moved us within one pound of the money, just to show you how tough it was. The majority of the field quit by noon with no fish. It was that bad. However, I like the fact that the first day leaders toughed it out to the last minute. If they hadn't caught that one 14-inch fish, they'd have dropped to second place. Good going, guys!

In spite of the cold and not finishing in the money, Alan and I had a good time fishing together and look forward to doing it again. I have now fished a tournament with all three of my sons and am definitely going to do some more next year.

Monday, October 6th

Sherry and I are cruising down I-90 on our way to Pierre, South Dakota for the first annual National Professional Anglers Association (NPAA) conference and photo shoot. I have several outdoor writers lined up to do interviews with, as well as shoot photos for upcoming articles. The NPAA was organized to help tournament anglers rise to a higher level of professionalism in their sport. I believe it is an organization that has been a long time coming and will be a great benefit not only to the angler, but to the whole fishing promotion industry.

Off season is a good time to enjoy pressure-free fishing and help out the youngsters. This is Christopher Gedwell with his first bass.

Sunday, October 12th

We had a productive time at the NPAA Convention the past six days. Sherry and I even had a rare opportunity to fish together and caught some nice walleyes, catfish and huge white bass, which she really enjoyed. Our catfish spot was a great hit with the writers, since a new catfish guide was being published in the spring and they needed articles and photos. I also had an opportunity to test drive the new fiberglass Fisher DV18 which will be my tournament boat next year. It was great!

Thursday, October 30th

It's cold and spittin' a little snow as I drive north into Minnesota and on up to Brainerd, where I'll be meeting Jim Kalkofen for another photo shoot, this time back at Ft. Peck, Montana. We did a shoot there last fall, and caught a lot of big fish. It should be a fun trip.

Thursday evening

I arrived in Brainerd at around noon, and Mike Simpson, who produces the In-Fisherman TV show, asked if I would be interested in going with him to catch some walleyes on the Mississippi River below the Brainerd dam. Al Lindner heard us talking about it and asked if he could come along, so we went down and caught a bunch of fish on jigs and minnows, but nothing big. Still, it was a fun day of fishing. When we got back, I headed over to Jim's house in Nisswa to load up the gear, get a short night's sleep, and make the drive to Montana in the morning.

October 31-November 7th

We pulled into Glasgow, Montana at about 6:00 p.m. on the 31st and had a dinner meeting with some of the local V.I.P.'s. Jim's friend, Greg, met us there and we talked strategy for tomorrow's fishing. It was agreed that we would try the same spots as last fall when we caught so many fish here. That is, unless the wind is blowing hard. Then we would opt for the river below the dam, which can produce some big fish this time of year.

The fishing proved to be phenomenal all the while we were here. We did some great photos of big lake trout, walleyes and saugers, then spent a day catching big northern pike out of the dredge cuts below the dam. The weather was perfect, with daytime temperatures in the 60's a couple of the days. As we were leaving, however, it was 10 degrees and snowing. It was time to put the boat away for the winter.

December

It's nice to be back home, resting up for the upcoming sportshow season. This is the time of year I work on my writing, as well as bookings for March and April speaking engagements. Sherry and I also work on reports to my sponsors and of course, it's contract renegotiation time as well. We have a pretty full schedule this coming year and are trying to get our taxes and all other paperwork finished as well. Since we publish both the Marquette and Green Lake County Visitor's Guides this time of year, that is keeping us––especially Sherry who sells the advertising—very busy through January.

Some Fort Peck lake trout, walleye and sauger caught while fishing with PWT director Jim Kalkofen.

Our son, Sean came from South Carolina to visit us over Christmas and left for the island of Haiti to see his fiancee' for two weeks before going back to finish his Master's Degree. They are getting married on the 4th of July in Maine, the only weekend I have free this summer. You know your schedule isn't flexible when your kids have to schedule their weddings around your tournaments!

Preseason 1998

February, 1998

We were home only four days this month, as we traveled the show circuit with the Walleye Information Center, manning the booth, giving seminars and talking with consumers about boats, motors and fishing tackle.

Our first three shows were in Cedar Rapids, IA; LaCrosse, WI and Duluth, MN., wrapping up with the Bass Pro Shops Spring Classic in Gurnee Mills, Illinois. Thanks to the weather pattern known as El Nino, we had snow-free roads the whole month, which is great when towing a boat from show to show.

These first three shows were kind of fun, as I had done these back in 1991. It was great to renew old acquaintances that I hadn't seen in several years, and to share the stage at each show with Danny and Juniors (At the Hop). Talking with them, I discovered that their schedule is worse than mine. They made me glad I was a pro fisherman and not a professional singer.

Babe Winkelman also worked these three shows, and it seemed like old times as we talked about the first time we met at a seminar at the Holiday Inn in Oshkosh back in 1980. I worked for him for a time in the mid-80's and I was on the Lindy-Little Joe pro team in 1988 when he was part owner. Babe and I go back a long ways and

I thank him for his role in helping me with my fishing career.

February finished up with seminars at the Madison Fishing Expo on the 28th. We had a packed house at the seminar, with more than 500 people coming to hear my talk on how forage base relates to fish location. The Expo is a great show to work, because it's all fishing. I've been doing that show for over 10 years.

March

The Expo wrapped up on March 1st with another seminar, and on the 2nd, I met Walleye Information Center director, Neil Hoyme in Portage where we traded booth components for our next shows. The Center is several boats and booths that are set up at 24 sportshows during the three-month show season. The new Fisher DV18 is displayed in the booth, and promotions are done for various sponsors of the booth. It is a great showcase for the sponsors, as well as for walleye fishing.

We set up Green Bay on the 5th and I think it was the first time I'd ever been there when it wasn't snowing. Actually, it had just stopped when we pulled into town. We weren't so lucky on Sunday

The winter is filled with dozens of seminars like this one at Norton's Dry Dock.

when it was time to head home, as a major blizzard shut down the airport and traffic was going nowhere. We decided to spend the night and try to make it home in the morning.

Monday, March 9th

It was still snowing this morning, but fairly light, although the wind was drifting the snow pretty bad. We loaded up and pulled out of town around 9:00 a.m. It was touch and go in a few places on the way back, but the roads were plowed pretty well. Still, it was interesting pulling the boat through the snowdrifts. I got a kick out of the looks on some people's faces as we drove through some of the towns. Pretty funny. I was supposed to speak at the county Historical Society meeting tonight, but they cancelled due to the snow.

I wrapped up the rest of March doing a seminar in Oconomowoc, Wisconsin on the 14th and my annual Norton's Dry Dock seminar on the 19th. The place was packed with standing room only, and I really appreciated the turnout. On the 21st I did another seminar at the Milwaukee Sentinel Sportshow, then took the Information Center up to Minneapolis and set it up at the show there. Actually, March

There's a huge amount of time to be spent in and around boats! A pro angler makes his living during this time of the year.

wasn't as busy as usual, and that was okay because April is really packed and my first tournament, the Walleye Super Pro, is only three weeks away. And I don't have my boat yet.

Friday, April 3rd

This is going to be a busy weekend. I'm speaking tonight in Monticello, Minnesota, which is about an hour north of Minneapolis, then tomorrow at Milwaukee at the Walleye University and finally, at Oshkosh on Sunday at another Walleye University event. It's my last major speaking of the season, then I have to get back home and rehearse for our church's Easter Drama (I play the preacher, what else?) which is Friday and Saturday. We'll attend Easter morning service on Sunday, then leave right from church for Lake Stockton, Missouri and the first tournament.

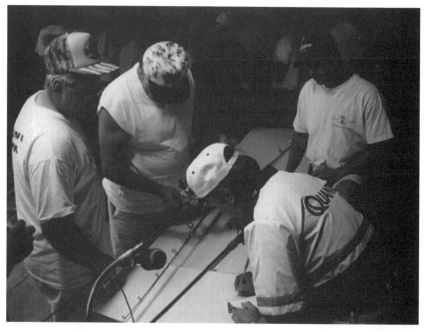

There are autographs to be signed at every event a notable pro attends.

1998 Walleye Super Pro Stockton, Missouri

Sunday, April 12th

It's Easter Sunday afternoon and we're on our way to Lake Stockton to fish the 1998 Walleye Super Pro. My boat is supposed to meet me there in the morning. Neil Hoyme and Dave Simmons from Fisher are rigging it right now. This will be the first time I've ever gone to a tournament without a boat, so I'm slightly uneasy to say the least. It was a busy winter, and I'm happy to be heading south for the first tournament.

Monday, April 13th

We were supposed to meet the guys from Fisher at the dock at 7:00 this morning. It's now 10 o'clock and they haven't gotten here yet. With only four days of practise and having never fished the lake before, I'm getting more uneasy all the time. I guess I'll just head back to the motel, get checked in, tie up some lines and tie up some spinner rigs, as I expect the bite to be similar to last year at Ouachita.

Monday evening

Neil brought me the boat at 2:30 this afternoon and I really appreciated his and Dave's hard work to get it ready for me. With only a few hours of daylight left, I decided to make a run down the lake and just look things over, punch in some spots that looked good and get back and put the finishing touches on the rigging.

After some last minute rigging, we got on the water at four o'clock and ran about 17 miles to a spot I had picked out on the map where the Little Sac River flows into the main reservoir. I was looking for some sand and gravel shorelines where walleyes would have spawned a few weeks ago, and found three good-looking spots. I was also looking for stained water up against flooded brush, and found some of that, too. There were only a few boats in the area, which I liked, so my plan is to come back tomorrow and fish these spots.

Tuesday, April 14th

Bernie Barringer pulled in this morning and he and I headed up into the Little Sac arm to fish those spots I found yesterday. We fished some flooded timber without success, and I decided to try a little shallower. We pulled into the first shoreline and Bernie caught a fish on the first cast. We caught three walleyes in 10 minutes, then left the spot. All of them were over the tournament size limit, which

Amateur partner Bill May and I are full of optimism as we head out for day one. Glory would be delayed, though.

is 18 inches on this lake. We continued to pick up more fish in similar-looking spots, which was flooded brush along pea gravel shorelines. All of the fish were males, and I hoped they would hold going into the tournament.

Wednesday, April 15th

Complaints are running high about the tough bite going on here, which is really encouraging. I caught two more walleyes today on two new spots and both were close to four pounds. I don't know what the spinner bite is doing, but by the sounds of all the complaining, it's not doing too well. Most of the guys are fishing in the Big Sac arm and I like that. They all know a few fish are being caught down there, so I don't expect to see many boats in the Little Sac come tournament day.

Thursday, April 16th

I told Mike Simpson about the bite I was on and he decided to take a gamble and have Dan Lindner fish with me today and film the technique I was using and explain how I located the fish. If I have a good tournament, he will use it as an opener to the show. We couldn't have picked a worse day to film with temperatures in the low 40's and a strong northwest winds ushering in, what else, a major cold front. We caught lots of bass, though, and I think I was pretty convincing that the walleyes were there as well. Of course, we didn't fish any of the spots I fished the last two days.

I'm expecting the bite to be terrible tomorrow. I only hope that I can put two or three fish in the boat to keep me in the hunt.

We pulled into the first shoreline and Bernie caught a fish on the first cast. We caught three walleyes in ten minutes, then left the spot. All of them were over the tournament size limit, which is 18 inches on this lake.

Friday April 17th, Day one of the Walleye Super Pro

ARGHHHHHHH! Not again! I really thought we would catch a few fish today, especially once the cold front passed and the water began to warm up in the afternoon. My partner, Bill May from St. Louis, Missouri and I fished our hearts out right up until the last minute. But the fish were gone, pushed deep because of the cold front. There were also no baitfish in the shallows, but we did catch plenty of bass, so I kept thinking (and hoping) the walleyes would move in and bite. They did not.

At least I wasn't alone, as two-thirds of the 45 all-time money winners came in skunked. Most of the other 16 had only one fish. Mark Brumbaugh is leading with a little over seven pounds, and I know he was fishing spinners. A few other guys had six pounds, then two fish, then a bunch of ones. This tournament isn't over yet. But I have to say that I really expected to catch fish today. In fact, I don't believe I've ever felt more confident about a tournament than this one, and I still do. I only hope that I can make up that seven pounds tomorrow. I know that Mark never caught a fish in practise, so I'm thinking he may not have that good of a day tomorrow.

Saturday, April 18th Day Two

My day-two partner was Rich Crannick from Overland Park, Kansas and we really had a great time today. It's amazing how much fun this is when you catch some fish! As we pulled into the first spot, I noticed shad jumping out of the shallow water, which told me the baitfish had moved back in. I was literally oozing confidence as we pulled up to the point and I caught a 19-inch walleye on the first cast. An hour later we had two more in the boat, and I was feeling pretty good about catching a limit today. But I made what could have been a critical mistake.

Instead of continuing to work the point and surrounding shallow shoreline, with three fish in the boat I decided to hit the two spots where I caught the two bigger fish on Wednesday. This took quite a bit of time and by the time we got back to our first spot, the shad had moved out and the walleyes along with them. I then decided to try one more spot where I had taken two fish the first day, and we boated our fourth and biggest fish at 3:00, only minutes before we had to come in. We then caught two more that were undersized and it was time to blast back to the weigh-in.

The bite seemed to stay pretty tough, as our four fish weighing eight and a half pounds put me in third place behind Brumbaugh who had two fish for a little over six pounds and Greg Horoky who came in with a limit and a huge weight of 14 pounds. I'm pretty sure

Television cameras tagged along almost every step of the way after I had one great day of prefishing. Everything worked out perfectly. In-Fisherman is the best in the business when it comes to covering these events.

had I stayed in my first spot, or had I gone to my last spot earlier, I would have had a limit of fish. With only one day to go, it's going to be tough to catch up, even if I take a limit tomorrow.

Sunday, April 19th, Day Three

Darin Lankford from Chilhowee, Missouri is my partner today. He fishes bass tournaments and knows how to handle a jigging rod. I think we need to catch at least one or two fish to make the money, and a limit of good fish for a chance to win. I talked with Horoky this morning and he was all smiles and full of confidence that the fish would be there. So was I.

We would be the fifth boat out this morning and Horoky would be the sixth. There's a great fog bank at the mouth of the harbor, but the main lake is clear. I told Darin that the Lord put that fog bank there so no one can see us make the quick turn into the Little Sac arm and follow us up there. He just smiled and said, "Let's go!"

The 200-horse Mercury roared as the flag was dropped and we disappeared into the fog. Banking right, we blasted through into bright sunshine as the shoreline sped by at a mile a minute. Horoky broke through the fog about a minute behind us as he sped toward the Big Sac arm. The next boat was a minute behind him and only a sliver on the water in the distance. We had made good our escape.

Now this might sound like I expected to be followed to my spot, but that's not necessarily so. The thing is, if a half-dozen or so boats fish the area that I'm fishing, they could take some good fish that I would have caught during the day. So I was hoping that I could get far enough up the arm to where the other guys couldn't tell which way I was fishing. As it turned out, we had the whole place to ourselves.

I felt good as we pulled up to the point where we caught three fish yesterday. The shad weren't jumping like yesterday, but the air was a cool 34 degrees, so I wasn't surprised. We worked the point hard for an hour and caught one 17 1/2-incher. It was time to move to the other spot, and try this one later when the shad moved in. As we were firing up the boat, the In-Fisherman film boat arrived. I showed them where I was going and pointed to where they could set up without drifting over the top of the spot. The next half hour was a zoo, and I'm going to relate it to you exactly how it all happened.

Darin and I eased up to within casting distance of the shore, and as I walked forward to drop the trolling motor in the water, Darin made a cast. Before I could set the trolling motor, he had a fish on and I quickly netted a 20-incher. As I put the fish in the livewell and turned on the switch, he made another cast and I got on the troller to keep us from drifting in too close. Just as I made my first cast he hollered "Got one!" and I ran back and netted a fat, 22-incher.

There were smiles all around as I picked up my rod and felt a solid thump on the other end. I set the hook, but the fish got off, and it felt like a good one. Seconds later, Darin hooked a really good fish that broke him off. That's two big fish in a row. It was time to settle down. We needed three more fish for a limit and this bite wasn't going to last forever. My next three casts produced three more fish. We had our limit! But was it enough?

As I was explaining the bite to the In-Fisherman crew, I noticed a shad skipping out of the water, indicating that it was being chased by a predator. I quickly cast to the spot, and was fast into a big fish. It turned out to be a 24-incher, which really gave our overall weight a boost. I was thinking that we had 13 or 14 pounds in the well and it was only 10:00 in the morning. We have all day to upgrade. I knew right then that I had a chance to win the tournament.

It was really interesting how the TV crew managed to film us catching all of our fish that day. That had never happened before, so I know that it's going to look good on TNN even if I don't end up winning the tournament. Right now, there's still Horoky and Brumbaugh, but I'm feeling good about at least finishing second or third.

As I was explaining the bite to the In-Fisherman TV crew, I noticed a shad skipping out of the water, indicating that it was being chased by a predator. I quickly cast to the spot, and was fast into a big fish. It turned out to be a 24-incher, which really gave our overall weight a boost.

3:30 p.m. Sunday afternoon

It's now 3:30 in the afternoon. We managed to catch three more walleyes after our limit, but couldn't upgrade what we had. The weather gradually warmed up to 70 degrees and the water was flat calm as we cruised our way in a full hour before we had to weigh. We are the first boat in with less than a half-hour to go. That means that Horoky and Brumbaugh don't have a limit or they would be in by now.

The tournament director and weighmaster checked our fish and declared them all alive (there's a 3/10ths of a pound penalty per dead fish). And it felt good that they were holding me back to weigh later, meaning they were pretty confident that I was in the top four or five. They will check other guys as they come in, and pull them to the side if they have a big weight. I hope there aren't too many of them. Sherry just came down to the dock and all I could say to her was "I got 'em".

The boats are coming in now, and I talked with quite a few guys and we pretty much know that Horoky only has one fish. I'm looking at no lower than second place. No one knows about Brumbaugh, but some guys are pulling in with some pretty good catches. Mike McClelland has pulled in alongside of me and Norb Wallock and Rick Olson have also been directed in. Olson has four fish with one 27-incher and a couple of other big fish. McClelland says I have 14 pounds and have won it. Even with Olson's big catch, he doesn't think it's enough to beat me. But we still have to weigh 'em!

4:10 p.m.

Brumbaugh still hasn't passed the staging area. Since the check-in is hidden behind the dock, he might just be back there putting fresh water on his fish.

It's 4:15 and Brumbaugh just came around the corner heading for the takeout dock! I see him drop off his amateur, which means he has no fish! Does that mean I've won?

The weigh-in is almost over. There's just Norb and Rick and me waiting to weigh, but we don't know for sure in what order. Mark Dorn comes down and tells Norb that he goes first, then he looks at my fish, shakes his head, looks at Rick's fish, looks back at me then tells Rick to go next. They are holding me for last. The last guy to weigh usually wins the tournament, and McClelland reminds me that Mark Dorn has only been wrong once. I remember it well. It was Mobridge a couple of years ago and I weighed last. I finished second.

Wallock weighs his fish and takes the lead with 19.54 pounds. Olson is next but can't beat Wallock. That means I need about 11

*There is no feeling in the world quite like this one! The win totalled
$51,500 including a Champion Boat with Mercury outboard, the
$1,000 Coleman Cool Under Pressure award and the T-H Marine Live
Release award.*

pounds to win. I'm sure I've got more than that, but I'm still waiting for the scale to prove it. As I walk up on the stage, Sherry gives me a thumbs up. When the basket is lifted to the scale, the crowd gasps, then applauds. Norb and I watch the digital read out: 14.07 pounds! I've won the Walleye Super Pro! Norb and I hug each other, then they hand me the first place trophy and a big fish to hold up for the photos. I'd been waiting for this moment for so long, that it hardly seemed real. The photos are shot and I call Sherry up on stage for more hugs. We cry. The emcee, Jim O'Rourke, hands me the microphone and asks what it's like to be the 1998 Super Pro Champion. Reality sets in and I am stunned. I turn from the crowd as tears fill my eyes. The crowd cheers, but I can't say anything. I am too overwhelmed.

Finally, I regain my composure. The emcee hands me the mike and walks off the stage. I call Sherry back over again and publicly thank her for her years of support and encouragement. The crowd cheers again. While they are cheering, she hugs and kisses me. They cheer some more. I tell them how much this means to me, after having five second-place and many more top-ten finishes the past 10 years. I tell them about Sherry crying on the way home from Ft. Peck last year, and how I was ready to quit.

Then I tell them about how I asked the Lord to bring the fish in shallow on the second day. My prayer was: "Lord, you created these fish and the Bible says that all the fish in the waters belong to you. If you make them come up here, I will make them bite." Within seconds, we caught our first fish, and the rest, as they say, is history. They applaud again.

I then share with them the faithfulness of God. I tell them that even if we walk away from Him, He says that He will never leave us nor forsake us. Forsaken is how I felt at the end of last season. But throughout the winter, God had shown Himself to be faithful in many ways.

You see, in the eyes of the world, I had to win the Super Pro to be called a winner. But in the eyes of God, I was a winner already, because I had accepted his free gift of salvation through his Son, Jesus Christ. To Him, I give all the glory for this victory. You see, even if I had never won, I could walk away knowing I had fished hard and done my best. Even if I had never won, I could still go to church on Sunday and sing praises to the Lord because He has given me eternal life.

But the win is nice, and it gives me a great opportunity to honor God for his goodness. It also gives me another chance to thank all of my sponsors who have supported me all these years, and especially the Saturday night prayer group at our church, who prays for Sherry and me every time we are on the road. Their prayers have been answered many times in many ways. I know that they were praying hard for me to win this tournament and I know that God will use it for His glory for many years down the road.

In addition to winning the $50,000 first place prize, I also won an additional $1000 for the Coleman Cool Under Pressure Award for the guy who moves up the most places after the first day; as well as the $500 T.H. Live Release Award. I was told that I was the first contestant ever to zero on the first day and win a PWT event. That's special, but a lot of other guys could have done that in this tournament. In fact, the top 10 guys all zeroed the first day, which shows you how tough it is to fish against these guys!

Monday, April 20th
After a long night of watching the victory on TV and visiting

My glory that day was shared by my amateur partner Darin Lankford. Darin jumped all the way to 8th place in the amateur division.

with friends, Sherry and I left Stockton at 4:00 in the morning, arriving home just before 5:00 p.m. in time to pick up our week's worth of mail. The phone machine is jammed with calls and the phone is ringing every five minutes. My turkey hunting season opens this week and I'm pretty fired up about that, too. I've got just over a week to get ready for Lake Erie, and I have to say that I'm not all that thrilled about it. I feel confident that I can catch fish there, but bad weather can really kill the bite, not to mention the equipment and contestants.

Monday, April 27th

I spent most of last week answering phone calls and reading mail, as well as getting a 24-pound turkey. The response to me winning the Super Pro has been unbelievable. I just can't believe the number of people who called to offer their congratulations. It's just really a blessing to know that people are genuinely happy for you and respect you. I had calls from people I hadn't heard from in years.

In Christian circles, you expect your friends and acquaintances to rejoice with you. After all, it is Biblical. But you don't always expect it from your worldly friends, your competitors. There are some who mock my Christianity, there are others who tolerate it, and there are those who don't agree with it, but respect it. This week I received calls and letters from all three groups and that's pretty humbling, knowing that these guys would take the time to call. I deeply appreciate that. To have their respect means more to me than winning the tournament, because I now know that they respected me even before I won the tournament and that means everything to me.

Eastern Pro/Am
Lake Erie
Port Clinton, Ohio

Wednesday, April 29th

It's early morning and Sherry and I are loaded up and heading to Grand Rapids where I'll be doing a seminar at the Christian Reformed Church for fathers and sons. We'll be staying overnight, then heading over to Port Clinton, Ohio in the morning for the start of practise in the Eastern Pro-Am on Lake Erie. The word is the bite isn't very good and that most of the fish have moved east out of the tournament boundary. We'll see.

Friday, May 1st

We made it in yesterday afternoon and got settled in to the LK Inn. The suburban was acting a little funny on the way down, and I wonder if I'm going to make it home. Rich Graves and Dan Toy from Red-D-Light Corporation, have been working on a sponsorship for a new suburban. I hope it comes through pretty soon. I really don't want to use my Super Pro money to buy a vehicle, as Sherry and I agreed if I ever won a big tournament, we would use the money to get debt-free. So far, we've paid off our second mortgage and credit cards, as well as some other bills accrued over 10 years of full-time tournament fishing. We even have a little left, but not enough to pay our first mortgage or buy a new truck. Guess I'll just have to go out and win another one!

I fished some of my old spots today and caught a limit of wall-eyes, but nothing spectacular. The water is really dirty around Green Island and Rattlesnake Island, due to strong winds and rain before we got here. Today, the water was calm, so fishing was pretty easy. My plan is to fish bottom bouncers and spinners with crawlers, since this is a proven winner on Lake Erie this time of year. I may take one day and troll crankbaits as well, just to see if the bigger fish are hitting them.

Saturday, May 2nd

I started the day over by Green Island, trying to fish the edge of the cleaner water. I ended up with a limit by noon, but there were at least 100 boats fishing the same area. I then went over to my favorite spot by Kelly's Island, which is straight north of the tournament takeoff site. The water was really clean there, and I caught a couple of bigger fish, but there didn't seem to be any great numbers of fish there. I fished spinners all day, and I think I'll spend the day around Kelly's tomorrow trolling crankbaits, looking for some bigger fish.

Sunday, May 3rd

It's the third day of practise, and I can tell that the bite is tough because the guys are launching early and spending long days on the water. The weather was beautiful, with calm seas, so I fished for 12 hours today, trying to put a big fish pattern together. I caught eight fish today, all on crankbaits, some were suspended at about 10 feet over 30 feet of water. Some were caught right off the bottom. It's been foggy and cloudy for the past three days, but it finally cleared today and is supposed to be clear and calm tomorrow. I'm going to give cranks a try again tomorrow and see what happens on a sunny day.

Monday, May 4th

Today was a perfect crankbait day: calm, sunny and easy to fish. I pulled cranks around Kelly's Island in 24-30 feet of water, trolling at every depth. Most of the fish I marked were about six feet off the bottom and should have been biting. I did lose two good fish, but never boated a walleye trolling. I switched over to spinners and fished back through those fish for two hours and caught a limit that weighed about 21 pounds. Gary Gray was fishing in the same area, pulling crankbaits and catching fish. He's really good at that and obviously was doing something different than I was. I've got one more day of practise and I'm concerned that I haven't put a real good plan together. I've caught a limit or more every day, but that usually isn't enough out here.

Tuesday, May 5th

I spent a couple of hours at Green Island today, then went up to Rattlesnake. There were a lot of boats, but it appeared the fish had really scattered and there weren't near the numbers of fish in either place as there was a few days ago. I then went over to Kelly's and caught a couple of fish right away on spinners. There are fewer fish on Kelly's, but they are bigger and seem to be biting pretty well.

Wednesday, May 6th, Day One

My partner today is Robert Plimpton from Sioux Falls, South Dakota. He likes to fish bottom bouncers and spinners, which is good, because that's what we'll be doing around Kelly's Island.

The conditions at Lake Erie can be treacherous, even life-threatening, but the average size of the fish is tremendous.

The weather was calm and a ton of boats went over toward Green. As it turns out, I'm glad I wasn't one of them. We went to Kelly's and started catching a few fish, almost went to Green, but decided to stay another hour. We then caught our limit and decided to stay the rest of the day and upgrade.

At noon, we pulled in a 7-pounder and didn't get another bite until 3:30 when we caught one about six pounds. That really helped our weight and we ended the day with five fish for 23.34 pounds, which puts me in there, but not very well. Ted Takasaki brought in 38 pounds, which is what you would expect for a weight at Erie. But he only caught five fish all day, and I don't expect this bite to get any better.

The guys who went to Green Island said the bite was terrible, that there were at least 300 boats there and only small fish were caught. I knew those fish were moving out of that area, so I'm really glad I didn't go there. Takasaki and Strochein both pulled big weights out where I was fishing, but they were a little bit deeper. Still, we caught eight fish today, which isn't great, and a couple of really good ones. We just needed to get a few bigger fish in the boat. Right now I'm right on the edge of the money cut, and I expect it to be around 60 pounds or so by the end of day three. Since Green turned so sour, I expect Kelly's to have a lot more boats on it tomorrow, and that's not good.

Thursday, May 7th

Chet Ratke from Riverside, Illinois was my partner today and we headed out to Kelly's on calm seas. The bite was really off for some reason all morning, but in the afternoon the wind began to pick up and so did the bite. As predicted, there were twice as many boats around us today than yesterday, but a lot of them left by ten o'clock with not many fish being caught. The fish started biting pretty steady at 2:00, unfortunately for us, we had to be in by 3:15, so we missed it. We caught two 7 1/2-pounders and one just under two pounds for a weight of 15.85. The last flight guys did really well, with all of them saying they caught their fish from one to four o'clock.

The wind is supposed to really pick up tomorrow and that means boat control will be tough. I'm not looking forward to running the eight miles out to Kelly's in that stuff, or trying to fish in it. If I can catch a limit tomorrow, I'll make the money for sure, and it will keep me in the hunt for the championship. We'll just have to see what the weather does.

Friday, May 8th

I'm going to say it here and now, that today wasn't a tournament competition, it was an ironman contest. My partner, Scott Ziegler from North Platte, Nebraska was as uneasy, as was I, as we pounded out to Kelly's in four- to five-foot waves. We caught a fish on the second drift, but our water was getting dirtier and dirtier. The waves continued to build all morning, and the boats that were out there with us kept going farther north into the wind, trying to get into cleaner water.

We heard a May Day call over the radio and could see a boat to the east of us waving a distress flag. So we pulled up our lines and headed over there, as did another boat. It was one of our tournament guys and his boat was filling with water. The other boat was Ron Creswell and he told me he would stay with them until the Coast Guard or PWT boat arrived. So we headed back out to fish, looked back and saw the boat go down. Ron and his partner fished the other two guys out and picked up as much of the floating tackle as they could. He said later that it was really tough pulling one of the guys into the boat in those big waves.

So we headed back out to fish, then looked back and saw the boat go down. Ron and his partner fished the other two guys out and picked up as much of the floating tackle as they could.

Both Scott and I were beginning to lose our nerve after witnessing that episode. My nerve left completely when we heard another distress call from a 24-footer that was going down with seven people on it. Fortunately, the Coast Guard was able to rescue them, but the boat was lost.

With the wind continuing to increase, all we could do was drift with it and put out two drift socks to slow us down enough to allow the spinners to work. The guys who were going farther north had their boats standing on end every time they went over a wave. Several were heading back to the dock early, and we decided that we weren't going any farther north, but that we would let the wind and waves drift us back toward the check-in.

Neither of us had the stomach to pound the two miles to the north. After the fiasco at Toledo two years ago, I promised my wife that I wouldn't take any more chances on Erie. In that one, I was 12 miles offshore when the wind suddenly picked up. I really thought that I wasn't going to make it back. Fifteen boats went down that day, and but for the grace of God we would have been the 16th. Scott fished that tournament and he agreed with me not to try a repeat performance today.

It is both my personal and professional opinion that with only a 115 boat field, we don't need to hold a tournament on a body of water this size. There are plenty of lakes we can fish with this small field without putting the fishermen in a dangerous situation. Fortunately, the guys used their heads and most of the boats held up, although a few others swamped. But everyone got back safely.

We never did catch another fish, ending up the day with only one 3-pounder. Gary Gray won the tournament with 87.38 pounds and the money cut (23rd place) was 62, about what I expected. There were a ton of weights in the 40's, and I finished up with 42 pounds. But my boat is in one piece and I'm only 15 pounds out of qualifying, which I can easily make up with three tournaments to go.

Lake Erie always produces big weights and big fish, and I really like fishing it when the weather permits. Back in 1993, I weighed in 112 pounds of fish in the PWT tournament. We had three calm days and the fishing was great. That was the year 10 of us finished in the Angler of the Year race with over 300 pounds of fish. No one has ever come close to that achievement since. But big water like Erie can be risky and I would rather see smaller total weights of fish, than have someone get badly injured or even killed fishing a tournament. It's just not worth the risk.

Saturday, May 9th

We're on the road heading home and my wife is trying to encourage me by saying I did the right thing by not going out farther to the north yesterday. I really don't need much encouragement about that decision. Sure, I would have liked to have caught a limit and made the money. Gary Gray was fishing up there, as were a couple other top 10 finishers. I'll give them credit. I just didn't have it in me.

We'll be home for a few days then head down to Columbia, South Carolina to attend Sean's graduation from seminary. We're really looking forward to the trip, I might even do a little fishing down there!

Sunday, May 24th

We're on a plane flying back from South Carolina and will get back late this afternoon, pack up, get a little sleep and head up to Leech Lake, Minnesota in the morning. South Carolina was beautiful and we had a great time. We picked up Sean's fiancee', Heather, who flew in from Haiti, finishing up her missionary trip, just in time for the graduation. I went fishing in Sparkleberry Swamp for shellcrackers, brim, redbellies and yellowbellies with a cane pole and crickets. It was great fun! I'd love to do it again sometime. But it's back to tournament fishing mode.

When fishing Lake Erie, sometimes getting back alive is enough to put a smile on your face. Having a basket of fish to weigh is just a nice bonus!

Central Pro/Am
Leech Lake
Walker, Minnesota

Monday, May 25th

The trip today was a repeat of last year, stopping in Superior to pick up leeches, then making our way up to Walker, Minnesota. They had an early spring this year, so I expect the fishing to be a little better than last year. Maybe Walker Bay will produce this year with the water being warmer. My plan going into prefishing is to really fish hard in Walker with slip sinker rigs and chubs, then pull spinners over by Ottertail and Stoney where I fished last year. I decided that I'm not going to do the sporting clays shoot this year, that my time would best be spent out on the lake.

Tuesday, May 26th

It was a beautiful, calm day today and I worked the humps in Walker Bay, stopping to fish whenever I graphed a big fish. I managed to catch only two of them, but both were over five pounds. There were a lot more guys fishing the Bay than last year, so I pulled out at noon and checked out some of the other hotspots from last year. I caught two more fish, one on a spinner and crawler and the other on a jigging spoon. My thoughts right now are to fish a few of the good humps on Walker Bay early, then cover water by pulling spinners along the weed edges to fill out a limit of fish.

Last year Pete Harsh was guiding during the tournament and he told me he caught several big fish out away from the boat pack at Ottertail. This year he's in the tournament and could be really dangerous. I checked some of the deeper stuff away from Ottertail today, but couldn't mark any fish out there. But the water is 10 degrees warmer than it was at this time last year, so those fish may have moved out of there.

Wednesday, May 27th

The wind blew hard today, which was supposed to make the fishing really great. It wasn't. I caught only three undersized walleyes and most of the guys I talked to had the same success, or lack thereof. The local people catch a ton of fish out of this lake through the ice, so I know they have to be here, but where? There's an awful lot of grumbling going on, especially by the guys who had a tough Erie tournament and need weight to get back into the championship. I expected the weed bite to be really hot, but all I see are small fish. That's disappointing. I thought there would be more fish in Walker Bay as well, but that isn't panning out either. I've got three days to figure this out and the wind is supposed to howl tomorrow bringing in a massive cold front. Oh goody.

Thursday, May 28th

We had another mini-tournament today similar to last year's. There were eight of us in the tournament and only three caught fish. I brought in a one-pound, 10-ounce walleye which gave me third place and $300. Steve Bissett had a 4-pounder and won. John Bergsma was second with a 3-pounder. I caught two other weigh fish as well today, with the largest coming from Walker Bay. The wind is supposed to keep blowing all night and the temperature is supposed to drop into the 30's by morning. There's not a whole lot of spots out of the wind on this lake, but I'll be looking for one tomorrow.

Friday, May 29th

I fished with Jim Kalkofen's daughter, Erika, today and man was it cold! With the strong winds, we went up into Kabakona Bay, a lake adjacent to Leech and in the tournament boundaries. Erika caught a nice 2 1/2-pound fish on a jig and leech, and I caught another one about 16 inches on the first reef in the bay. That turned out to be it for the day. I'm not planning to fish this lake in the tournament unless the wind really starts to blow. The channel from Kabakona to Leech also has some small fish, especially in the early morning under the bridge, but the guys staying on Kabakona know about these spots and I expect at least a few of them to fish them right away in the morning on the first day. I hope this wind dies down so I can work some spinners deep off of Ottertail tomorrow.

Saturday, May 30th

I took Sherry out to dinner last night to celebrate our anniversary and the buzzword from the locals was that the fish were biting good after dark and just before sunrise. That means the lake is on a night bite and that by tournament hours, they shut down. The best bite is early morning for about an hour, so I need to be on my best spot right away in the morning. The problem is, I don't have a best spot right now.

Saturday, May 30th

It always amazes me how fast time goes. I mean, five days of practise seems like a lot, then all of a sudden it's the last day and you still don't have a program together. This morning it's pouring down rain. I just got the boat in the water when the storm hit. I'm going to unhook my trailer and go have breakfast. I better turn on my bilge pump before I go, or everything will be floating in the boat when I get back.

The rain hung on until about 11 o'clock, and several guys who went out early are back in already. I'm just heading out. I've got about four hours to check out some spots and there are a couple of humps in Walker Bay that I haven't fished yet, so I want to at least check them out and put them on my GPS for backup spots close to the weigh-in.

I managed to do what I needed to in the short time I had today. I

I expected the weed bite to be really hot, but all I see are small fish. That's disappointing. I thought there would be more fish in Walker Bay as well, but that isn't panning out either. I've got three days to figure this out and the wind is supposed to howl tomorrow bringing in a massive cold front. Oh goody.

actually had one big fish on, but it got off. I assume, by the way it fought, that it was a walleye. High winds are forecasted for tomorrow, so my plan is to start in Kabakona Bay where it won't be as windy, then work back out in the main lake if and when the wind dies down.

Sunday, May 31st, Day one

It's 4:30 a.m. and the northwest wind is already 30 miles per hour. I'd be real surprised if they cancelled the tournament day, so I'm launching the boat and tying it off, then going for breakfast. The flags are sticking straight out and the waves are even big in Walker Bay. I saw one boat come across and he was pounding pretty hard. I'm not looking forward to going out there, not after the last day at Erie.

Sunday noon

The takeoff was delayed hour-by-hour and the tournament day finally cancelled at 11 o'clock. Most of the guys are okay with it and some are downright jubilant, but others are pretty upset, especially the tough old guys from Minnesota and South Dakota who fish in this stuff all the time. I'm more puzzled than anything, since these waves aren't even close to what we had the last day on Erie and all of us are fishing close to shore if anything would happen.

The explanation we got was that the Erie waves were rollers and these Leech Lake waves were closer together and more dangerous. I'll go along with that, except I'll never be convinced that the Erie waves weren't as dangerous. I have mixed feelings, since I could have fished a few of my spots and maybe caught some fish, while a lot of the other guys wouldn't have been able to effectively fish their spots. Also those who are 15 to 20 pounds out of qualifying really need this extra day. I think Jim and Mark made the right call here. After all, safety should come first. I only wish they would have done it the last day at Erie as well. But we're having a two-day tournament, so everyone is equal. I'll keep my first day partner tomorrow, Nicholas Luciano, from Minneapolis.

Some of the guys trailered up to Lake Winnie and fished up there today, while others had a sunfish tournament off the road in one of the bays. I decided it would be a good day to catch up on my sleep and clean the boat. I also went shopping with Sherry, which I never do.

Monday, June 1st, Day two

The winds are 20-25 m.p.h. out of the west-southwest and are supposed to blow in some pretty good thunderstorms today. With the wind as strong as it is, I've decided to go to Kabakona Bay, at least for awhile, then into the main lake around Stoney Point or Ottertail.

Monday evening

Whew! What a day. We motored into Kabakona and Tommy Skarlis was working the bridge channel, so I kept going to the first reef where Erika caught that nice fish. The wind was howling and it was tough to hold on the break, but we fished the whole edge for two hours and caught a couple of northerns, but no walleyes. Skarlis pulled out from the bridge just before we were ready to leave, so we spent about 15 minutes there and caught a couple of short fish before heading out to the main lake. I knew the wind would be honkin' on Walker Bay, so we went right through it over to the backside of Stoney and pulled spinners and bouncers along the weededge, catching short fish and finally getting one that measured.

By early afternoon, the skies were really threatening and lightning was everywhere. We decided to take the south route back through Walker Bay and pull into the check-in, wait out the storm and then go back out if time permitted. We got back in and the lightning seemed to be farther east, but the Sheriff's Department had tornado warnings out. I knew of a small hump up the lake only two miles away, and decided to risk it.

We just got to the spot when it started to rain, then the worst lightning I've ever seen began to flash all around the boat. We caught two quick fish, but sparks were flying off our graphite rods and Nick was getting a little nervous. So was I.

We just got to the spot when it started to rain, then the worst lightning I've ever seen began to flash all around the boat. We caught two quick fish, but sparks were flying off our graphite rods and Nick was getting a little nervous. So was I. I had been hit by lightning fishing a tournament on Mille Lacs several years ago, and I wasn't relishing a repeat performance. I decided it was past time to get out of there, so we blasted back just as the worst hail I've ever been in began to pound the boat and the wind cranked up to 60-70 miles per hour. This was ugly stuff, and I knew some boats would be late getting in.

Our three fish weighed a whopping 3.17, but with only 12 pounds leading the tournament and a whole bunch of zeroes and one fish, I knew I had a good chance to not only cash a check, but if things went right, to win the tournament. That meant I had to fish Walker Bay and hope to get the right five or six bites from the big fish that were scattered out in the deep water off the humps. I only caught two of them in practise, but it was my only chance to get back in it. Since two of our fish today came off of one of those humps, I felt that we could catch some small fish along with at least a couple of big ones to get in the money. We also had a good shot at cashing a

Three small fish was our catch, each barely making the minimum measurement. All PWT events have a 15-inch minimum, unless state law requires that it be longer.

big fish check. Since we caught our fish on a slip-sinker rig and redtail chub, that was the plan for tomorrow.

Tuesday, June 2nd, Day three

My partner today was Roger Combs from Dayton, Ohio and we went to my best hump on the north end of Walker Bay. We graphed the hump and marked one good fish on the edge, so I tossed the buoy and set up so that we could drift into the fish, which was no problem with the 25 m.p.h. northwest winds. It was brutally cold and sleet was coming down, but the 5.79-pound walleye sucked in the chub and Roger did a great job with the net in the bouncing boat.

It was just the first hour and all I could think of was that I needed three or four more bites like that to win the tournament. We continued to fish the reef hard, catching undersized walleyes. After two hours, I decided to make a run to a south hump that I had caught some small fish on.

Another boat was there when we pulled up, but they were on the far side, about 100 yards away. I figured we'd just fish the far point, but the other contestant had a marker buoy on it and I didn't feel comfortable fishing by his marker, even though he was a long way away from it. So I moved away and started graphing a sliver that came off the point, when he motored over by me. I recognized him as Dan Stier and figured I might be in for a butt-chewing. Instead, he invited me to fish his marker, since he knew I had prefished the spot, while he would continue to fish the other end. What a class act!

I knew that Dan was in a position to win the tournament and I didn't want to interfere with his spot, but he insisted that I stay, so I worked the tip, marking one nice fish, but not getting it to bite. About five minutes later, Brian Ney pulled in and started fishing, moving toward the point. We chatted a little bit and he said he could have won the tournament with the fish he'd lost. That hurts. I said, "Maybe you can catch that one on the tip. Dan and I both fished it and it won't bite." Two minutes later, as he crossed the point, I saw his rod bend and he hauled in a nice 4 1/2-pounder. All Dan and I could do was laugh.

I was really hoping to take another good fish off this spot, which I later learned was where Dan and Brian fished yesterday and most of today, both finishing 10th and 12th respectively. I figured that three boats were a little much on this hump, so I decided to head back to the north hump, graph it, and hope to mark a couple of big fish. It didn't happen. The wind was blowing harder and harder and we kept checking as many deep breaks as we could find in Walker Bay. We caught a few more short fish, but that early morning big fish was it for the day. The fish did earn us a big fish award and $1,000, but one more like it would have put us in 13th place.

My good friend, Pete Harsh, won the tournament, fishing the exact spot he told me he had fished last year and caught all those nice walleyes when he wasn't in the tournament. He is one tough fisherman, back trolling into that awful wind in the main lake. He certainly deserved it. His winning weight was 22.60 pounds and the money cut was 12.47. I should have made the money in this one. I let it get away on the first day, when I didn't fish Walker Bay until the last half hour. These tough tournaments are the ones I usually do

This day-three 5.79-pounder wasn't enough to move me into the money, but it sure helps towards making the championship.

well in, and I was a little disappointed in myself for not fishing a better tournament mentally.

Thursday, June 4th

We made it back home late last night, after stopping at the New Jerusalem Church in Canton, Minnesota to speak at a father/son dinner. It was great to be home, but I'll be guiding for the next three days, doing a group nature tour of the county. Sean came home a couple of days ago and we're finalizing plans for his upcoming wedding on the 4th of July. My son, Steve and I will be fishing the 300-boat Mercury Nationals that I emceed last year, and will start prefishing in a few days. It's good to be back home, and fishing home waters, even though my finishes on Lake Winnebago have been feast or famine.

Good friend Pete Harsh won the event. Pete was guiding during the Leech Lake tournament the previous year. He won by fishing the same spot where he'd been guiding.

Monday, June 8th

Rich Graves called today and said that my new suburban was ready! He and Dan Toy would meet me in Fond du Lac tonight so I can have it ready at the Mercury Nationals. What a huge blessing to retire my old blue suburban that served me faithfully the past nine years! I'm so grateful to Red-D-Light for their sponsorship. The suburban looks really great!

Mercury Nationals
Lake Winnebago, Wisconsin

Saturday, June 13th, Day one

Steve and I spent the better part of the past three days searching for walleyes on Lake Winnebago in preparation for the Mercury Nationals. We found three reefs that had respectable fish on them, but whether or not they would be big enough to win was debateable. We caught all of our fish in practise jigging with half crawlers and leeches on the edges of the reefs, with some fish coming off the top, and that was the ticket today. We finished the first day with a limit of six fish and 12 pounds, which put us close, with 16 pounds leading. We knew we needed to duplicate that tomorrow, if we were going to have a shot at winning or at least making the top 10.

Sunday, June 14th, Day two

Today was cloudy and calm, a perfect day to work our reefs. Unfortunately, the fish didn't cooperate. I just couldn't believe that these fish were here all week and just vanished on Day Two. I don't know why I'm always so mystified by this. After all, it isn't like this is the first time walleyes have done such a thing, especially in a tournament. It is awful frustrating, though. I really wanted to do well in this tournament with Steve, since we made the money last year in the MWC tournament. Here's a lake with over one million walleyes in it and we can only catch one fish. As Steve would say: "What's up with that?!"

In spite of the tough day, it was great fishing with my son before heading out to Lake Oahe for the third PWT qualifier. We had fun the first day, and even the second day, with both of us trying to figure out what happened to the fish. I know it gave Steve a better appreciation of what I go through doing this every other week.

A brand new Suburban, sponsored by Red-D-Light, ready to launch the boat for the Mercury Nationals on Lake Winnebago.

Midwest Pro/Am
Lake Oahe
Pierre, South Dakota

Thursday, June 18th

We drove hard all day to make the 650-mile trip to Pierre, South Dakota and beautiful Lake Oahe. Sherry and I are both excited about this week, because I've done pretty well on this lake and it's also the week before we head out to Maine for Sean and Heather's wedding. My guess is Sherry's a little more pumped up about the wedding than she is about the tournament. I'm currently only 17 pounds out of qualifying and that's certainly doable out here.

Friday, June 19th

I like fishing slip-sinker rigs and chubs for big walleyes on this lake, and that was my plan today. The wind was really crankin' this morning, so I decided to work some of the south stuff toward the dam, but not the real good humps that I fished last year. I'm saving those for later in the week. As it turned out, I caught quite a few fish today, including a couple of 5-pounders, which tells me that there are some decent fish on the south end of the reservoir.

One of the most popular spots is the main point off Chantier Creek (locally know as Shanty), but there were several boats on it and the creek arm itself was loaded with boats. I really like that main point, but I don't think it'll be available come tournament morning. There's room for one boat, at least the best spot on it, maybe two or three at the most fishing each side of the point. I don't like guys fishing that close around me, so I'm going to pass on it, maybe catch it on the way in if I'm fishing farther south.

Saturday, June 20th

More wind again this morning and a local tournament going on to boot. Most of the boats fished south and were working almost every spot I fished yesterday. Dip nets were flying in every direction, and I wondered if there would be any fish left by the end of the day. I worked my way down to the dam and checked out some of the humps in Corps Bay. I marked some pretty good fish, dropped a line down and caught a nice one in 40 feet of water. I hate fishing that deep, but sometimes that's where they're hanging out this time of year. I continued to catch a fish or two in almost every spot I stopped and I'm leaning more and more toward fishing the south end. I do need to check out my north spots from the past, however,

Sorting out the best crawlers. It takes a lot of nightcrawlers to fish a whole week on these western reservoirs.

and spending two days up there leaves me only one more day to put this together in the south.

This is a real dilemma. I don't want to miss what's happening up north and I need to check it out. But I have found fish south and could really use a couple of days to fine tune my presentation, as well as find more spots in case the ones I fish the first morning don't produce. Decisions, decisions.

Sunday, June 21st

The local tournament was won with 24 pounds for seven fish, and those came from the south, which is a decent weight. However, another tournament held up north was won with 42 pounds for seven fish, so guess where I'm heading to today! I know of a bunch of good spots up there as well as way up into the Cheyenne River. That's a long haul, but 200 horses will get me there in a hurry.

Catching a few nice fish in practise is always encouraging, but when they leave you in the tournament, it's doubly frustrating.

Sunday evening

I pulled in at 7:00 tonight with about a pint of gas left in the boat. In fact, I switched over to my 10 gallon auxiliary tank and the needle is frozen on empty. I gas up at the resort and it takes 39.8 gallons. Both tanks combined hold 40, so I'm glad I didn't run any farther north. I never did make it way up the Cheyenne today, but I covered a lot of water and caught tons of walleyes, except they were kind of on the small side. If it's calm tomorrow morning, I'm going all the way to Fish Gut Creek in the Cheyenne River. I did really well up there a few years ago, and I doubt if very many boats will make that long run with some decent fish biting close. It would be nice to have a spot like that all to myself if I can catch a 3- to 4-pound average.

Monday, June 22nd

It's 5:00 a.m. and the lake is flat calm, so I'm going to make the run up to the Cheyenne. Once committed, I'll have to spend the day, or pull in and gas up somewhere on the way back. I'm questioning whether this is such a good idea, but a honey hole away from the crowd is worth the run, providing we don't get a big north wind on one of the tournament days.

Monday evening

I was right about one thing: there weren't many boats that far up, although I actually had three boats run farther up the Cheyenne than I did. Did they know something, or were they just out looking around? I guess we'll find out in a couple of days. I wasn't impressed with the bite up there, catching only a few fish on some really good points. I fished my way back, pulling into the dock at 5:00 p.m. I've got one day left and I wish I hadn't gone north today. It seems like I wasted the whole day and could have put it to better use fine tuning my presentation down south. Since tomorrow is everyone's short day, I expect the south end to get fished pretty hard, and I sure don't want to show anyone where I'm going to be fishing.

Tuesday, June 23rd

Sometimes a guy can get really stupid and I plead guilty to that today. A good friend of mine told me there was a good bite on big fish going just south of the Cheyenne where we caught fish in a tournament last year. So I blasted back up there today instead of going south, figuring that I already knew the south end well enough and it was important to check this out. The gas guys at the resort really like me! As it turned out, I did catch some decent fish in 40 feet of water, but I saw the guy who told me about the fish he caught yesterday and he had a look on his face like somebody shot his dog. "This spot was loaded with fish yesterday. Where'd they all go?," he asked, almost pleading with me to give him an answer. I had no clue. All I knew was that I had wasted my last day of practise and I know better than that. I would fish south in the tournament, but I didn't feel very prepared. And that's not a good feeling.

Wednesday, June 24th, Day one

My decision to go south and fish the deep humps in Corps Bay didn't pan out. My amateur partner David Doretti from Scottsdale, Arizona and I managed to catch a limit of small fish for 8.37 pounds, but we couldn't put a decent fish in the boat. There were more boats fishing the humps than I expected and a few of them caught some bigger fish than we did. We worked the 40-foot depth and kept catching small fish and I'm wondering where the big fish went. I'm be-

Oahe is an oasis in a barren prairie. Despite its immense, foreboding size, it's loaded with walleyes and a great place to fish.

ginning to see my chance at making the championship slip away. I need a big weight the next two days for sure.

Thursday, June 25th, Day two

More small fish. I have to say that I am totally mystified as to what happened to the bigger fish. There's tons of baitfish around these humps and the bigger walleyes should be here. Something just isn't right and I can't put my finger on it. These humps are consistent producers of big fish this time of year and there's very little boat pressure. Why aren't they here? Greg White from Rapid City and I weighed another six-fish limit for only 7.89 pounds. Gary Parsons is leading and I know he's fishing somewhere close by.

I've been doggedly fishing these humps, hoping the big fish will move in and turn on. Because of that, I haven't had a chance to fish any of the spots where I caught fish the first couple of days, thinking I'll probably end up with the same size fish anyway. I re-

It's always a pleasure to bring a limit of fish to the scale, but these aren't the right fish to put me in the money or make the championship.

ally wanted to hit the main point at Shanty, but when I went by on the way back to the check-in, there was a boat on it, so I just kept going. I did stop at one and there was a boat netting a pretty good fish. The guy later told me that he took two 4-pounders off of that point in the last 10 minutes and that he got there about a minute before I did. Ouch.

Friday, June 26th, Day three

My partner today was Randy Pearpoint from Regina, Saskatchewan and we went back to the same spot. I was kind of feeling like the guy who keeps hitting himself in the head with a hammer because it feels so good when he stops. The scenario was the same when we got there, small fish in 40 feet of water. At noon, I decided to move out into 50, then 55, then 60 feet and there they were! We caught three bigger fish before it was time to come in and I was physically and mentally sick that I hadn't checked the deeper water the first day. I knew those fish had to be there someplace and my stubbornness to stay at 40 feet probably has cost me making the championship. I had the right spot and the proper technique, but because I don't like fishing in real deep water, I couldn't force myself to look any deeper than 40 feet.

This was a lesson well learned and a mistake that won't be repeated. Gary Parsons won the tournament spending all three days parked on that main point on Chantier Creek. That news made me even sicker. Not that Parsons won, but that he won it on that point that I had dismissed because I thought it would be fished too hard. One of the other top five guys caught all their fish on the next point past FishGut Creek, about a mile past where I stopped to fish in practise.

Right now I'm feeling really snakebit, yet I've been close to having three good tournaments in a row. It's amazing how the little things can keep a guy from performing well. As I said before, this is more of a mental game than anything else, and at least in the last two tournaments, mental mistakes have cost me. Last year, I was really discouraged about this time and even though I'm sitting way out of qualifying for the championship, I'm fairly upbeat about it. I'm probably going to have to win Ft. Peck to make the championship cut of 40, or at least make the top two or three. Sometimes it's good going into a tournament in desperation. With nothing to lose, you fish a little bit looser.

One thing I know for sure, my mental block of not fishing deeper than 40 feet has been removed forever. Had I prefished that deep, I would have caught some of those big fish, which would have given me the confidence to fish deeper in the tournament. It was a pretty foolish mistake for someone who's fished walleyes for almost 45 years. Once again, I learned something, which I do in every tournament I fish.

Sherry and I will stay the night, then get up early and head for home. We had our neighbors pick up all our mail so we can go through it when we get home on Sunday, since we will be heading to the airport early Monday morning to fly to Bangor, Maine for the wedding. One nice thing about the long drive back from South Dakota is that there is plenty of time to get all of the "what if's" out of my system. We're looking forward to Maine, since we've never been there before, and to having a feeding frenzy on lobster.

Wednesday, July 8th

We pulled in from Maine late last night after being stuck at the Newark, New Jersey airport for half the day. Right off hand, I can think of at least 1,000 better places to be stuck in for a day, a dentist's chair is one that comes to mind. When we got to Milwaukee airport our car battery was dead, so we waited another hour for AAA to come and jump it. We finally got home at about 10:00 p.m. totally exhausted.

The wedding was great. Sean is our youngest of five children and the last to get married. His wife, Heather, is wonderful and we are so happy that he found such a great wife. Before and after the wedding, Sherry and I took a couple of whale and puffin tours, which was really neat. The whales were cool to watch and we saw a very rare right whale that came up right next to the boat. I enjoyed the seabirds and just being on the northeast coast for the first time. The lobsters took a real beating from us all week. I never realized how many ways lobster can be cooked. It was decadent!

Maine was great, but we were ready to come home and get back into the fishing mode. I have a seminar at Lake Arrowhead Campground on Lake Puckaway on Saturday and it's always well attended. Since I used to guide on the lake and still fish it when I can, it's fun to talk about my old stompin' grounds again. The lake produced my biggest walleye ever, a 14-pound, 4-ouncer back about 30 years ago. I also caught a 14-pound, 4-ounce walleye in Lake Tobin,

Saskatchewan during the Vanity Cup tournament a couple of years ago. I'm not that big on fishing for big walleyes, I just like to wall-eye fish. Catching 16-inchers is just as much fun to me as catching 10-pounders. Unless, of course, it's during a tournament!

Western Pro/Am
Fort Peck Reservoir
Glasgow, Montana

Wednesday, July 15th

It's 2:30 a.m. and Sherry is packing the suburban with her "travel food" while I hitch up the boat. Our plan is to make the 1,000 mile drive straight through to Ft. Peck, then have all day Thursday to visit with our friends Chris and Jean Christensen (no relation) who provide us with bait for the tournaments and photo shoots every year. The rest of the day will be spent at bait shops getting the scoop on the bite. The Governor's Cup is this weekend and once again, some good weights are expected close to the weigh-in site.

Friday, July 17th

Today was the first day of practise and the weather was picture perfect, so I decided to make the run up to the area of Hell Creek where the tournament was won last year. After bombing out on the spoon bite last year, I'm going to stick with bottom bouncers and spinners and work the shallow weed edges in stained water at about eight to ten feet deep.

That's exactly what I did today, and was pretty impressed. I caught one over 10 pounds and several other nice fish. I had to try a spoon and caught two on it, one 7-pounder. But I think the spinners are the way to go, and I also think that I need to stay in the main arm, even though the Dry Arm has been producing some decent fish. I won't discount it yet, but I probably won't fish it until the last day of practise.

The first day leaders of the Governor's Cup fished Haxby Point, which is the first long point coming out of the Dry Arm. I didn't want to hear that, especially since I found so many good fish up at Hell Creek. I really need to go back up into that area and find more spots holding fish. I've always been a structure fisherman and try to work small areas thoroughly, rather than pull spinners on long stretches of shorelines. But that can win this tournament, and I'm going to have to go against the way I like to fish and try that, which is hard for a guy who's almost 50 and set in his ways.

Fort Peck produces some beautiful walleyes. A limit of these each day would vault me into the championship.

Saturday, July 18th

Because the Governor's Cup is going on, I decided to make the run way up out of their tournament boundaries so I wouldn't be on any of the contestant's fish. I went up into Snow Creek and fished several good points, then ran to our tournament boundary and worked my way back, pulling spinners down long stretches of shoreline. I caught some decent size fish today, but wasn't impressed with the numbers. I did find a couple of spots holding a ton of 15-inchers, so I punched those into my GPS for emergency fish. But that won't cut it in this one. I expect it to take 70 pounds to win, maybe a little more. I need a six-fish limit of 4- to 5-pounders a day to win this thing.

Sunday, July 19th

I made the run up to the Sutherland Arm, which is a big creek channel across from Hell Creek. It was pretty windy, so I ran clear to the back end, about three miles and fished my way back out. The water was pretty dirty, but the fish were really in there. I caught several in the 3- to 4-pound class and this area, combined with my spots at Hell Creek could win it for me. I fished a couple of other points on the way back and caught fish off of them as well. I'm not seeing a ton of boats, and wonder where everyone is at. It's a big reservoir, however, and it doesn't take much to hide 115 boats.

Monday, July 20th

Since Sutherland was so good yesterday, and my plan was to fish there the first tournament day, I decided to recheck the spots at Hell Creek and watch the mouth of Sutherland to see how many guys fish up there today. As it turned out, there were more boats in there than I had hoped, and being in the last flight, I wondered if I would have a spot when I got up there. Also, I fished my Hell Creek spots and never had a bite, which is not a big surprise on this reservoir. It has a history of

The water was pretty dirty, but the fish were really in there. I caught several in the 3- to 4-pound class and this area, combined with my spots at Hell Creek could win it for me. I fished a couple of other points on the way back and caught fish off of them as well.

piles of fish on a spot one day, and nothing the next. My confidence was slipping as I finished off the day point-hopping back to the boat ramp.

Tuesday, July 21st

It's the last day of practise and I fished with the local game warden today. I decided to stay close, since the winds are really strong, and I wanted to fish the first couple of points up in the Dry Arm. We caught an 8-pounder right off the bat, then caught another one about five. A couple of boats came in, probably to get out of the wind. Reggie Theil was there and he hadn't done well all week, but caught a couple here, so he's planning to fish here tomorrow.

We moved farther up the lake and caught fish in a couple of other spots. I then decided to throw my prefishing out the window and come in here the first day. Here we go again. I got burned doing that last year, but I think there's winning fish here if there aren't too many guys fishing it. Also, it's only a few miles from the boat ramp and that gives me at least an hour and a half to two hours of extra

Optimism rules, you can see it on the faces of myself and my day-one partner John Janousek.

fishing time. I actually feel good about this decision. I hope I still do after tomorrow.

Wednesday, July 22nd Day One

Ah, the best laid plans of mice and men! My first day partner was John Janousek from Hutchinson, Minnesota and as we came around the corner of Haxby Point, there were five other boats there. I couldn't believe it! We moved away from them and set up our spinner rigs and covered the area like a blanket. Three of the five boats were guys that were in the top 10 for Angler of the Year and the other two were Reggie Theil and Larry Mote.

There didn't appear to be much of a bite going, as we could easily see most of the boats and would have seen any fish being caught.

After an hour of working the best spot with no luck, we began to point-hop, but there was just nothing happening. I decided we needed to graph out in deeper water (see, I did learn something from Oahe) but unfortunately, we didn't mark any fish. Where in the heck did they go? I was determined not to die on these spots, so at noon we started hitting other spots and finally caught six small fish off of one of the points that I fished last year. They only weighed 7.72 pounds, but a lot of guys had a tough day, so I can still make it to championship with a couple of 25-pound days. That's not going to be easy out here, but if those big fish come back, it is possible. Both Larry Mote and Reggie Theil caught some nice fish on that point in the afternoon, so maybe they're coming back in. Let's hope so.

As we came around the corner of Haxby Point, there were five other boats there. I couldn't believe it! We moved away from them and set up our spinner rigs and covered the area like a blanket. Three of the five boats were guys that were in the top 10 for Angler of the Year.

Thursday, July 23rd. Day Two

The weather was calm today, which made for easy fishing. My partner was Jon Johnson from Richfield, Minnesota, and we were the first boat to the point today, which was really encouraging. We really worked it hard, but nothing was happening. I wasn't going to wait until noon today to move, especially since it was my short day. We blasted across the lake over to Bear Creek and fished the same type of points. I stuck a really big fish, but it got off. We caught some short ones, but no keepers. With only a little time left, we went back to the point where I caught the fish yesterday and caught one fish that weighed 1.71 pounds. That was it.

Well, I now knew where I was at, sitting in 97th overall for the year and needing at least 40-plus pounds to get in. A 40-pound weight is huge in any tournament, but it would be a real miracle here. Now my goal was to finish in the top 75 for the year, because that's the cut for getting invited to fish next year. I need a decent day to even do that, but there's also that Pinnacle $25,000 big fish bounty to go for, so I'm really motivated to fish hard tomorrow.

Friday, July 24th

The wind was really crankin' this morning, so I decided to head over to Bear Creek instead of Haxby and I caught a fish right away.

Waiting for a blast-off, it's amazing to look around and see the top walleye anglers in the world and a half-million dollars worth of state-of-the-art walleye rigs all in one place.

Andrew McClary, Ft. Morgan, Colorado was my partner and at 8:00 o'clock, we had another fish in the boat. Things were really looking up and I thought, "Oh boy, here we go." We continued to work the point, but nothing else was cookin' so we worked our way to the west and pulled into Haxby with about two hours of fishing time to go and still only two small fish.

There was no one at Haxby, which was good, and we set up and I stuck a real nice fish, probably five or six pounds right away. Unfortunately, it got off. I was sick. Andrew was really encouraging, though, and we made another pass through the spot and caught a 5-pounder. Reggie Thiel was going by and told me he had a limit and that the fish were just stacked in here early this morning. That pretty much summed up my year with the exception of the Super Pro. Every time I zigged and should have zagged. Oh well, I knew that the weight I had today, 7.91 pounds, would move me up overall, but I doubted I would be in the top 75.

Scott Fairbairn's comeback was the greatest in walleye tournament fishing history and it's doubtful it will ever be repeated. That kind of day gives encouragement to all of us. As long as the bait's in the water and there's time on the clock, don't ever give up.

After that great start, winning the Super Pro, I ended up finishing 88th overall. The PWT is guessing that at least 15 guys will drop out of fishing next year's circuit, since they are adding two more qualifiers, making it six tournaments. So I'm probably going to be invited anyway. There won't be a Super Pro event in 1999, which keeps me the reigning Super Pro Champion for another year. The new format will be to invite the top 75 pros from 1998, with the top 30 finishers in 1999 going to the championship. The circuit will be split into two divisions, with three qualifying tournaments in each division. Ten additional anglers will come from the two divisions as well as this year's champion and amateur angler of the year to round out the championship field.

Ft. Peck ended with a bang, actually, more like an explosion, as Scott Fairbairn jumped from 49th place after day two, to win the tournament with almost 38 pounds of walleyes. That huge weight also won him Angler of the Year by a half-pound. It was the greatest comeback in walleye tournament fishing history and it's doubtful it will ever be repeated. That kind of day gives encouragement to all of us. As long as the bait's in the water and there's time on the clock, don't ever give up.

John Hook also had a pretty good day, boating a 12.19 walleye that won him the Pinnacle PWT record walleye, cashing a check for $25,000. Talk about an emotionally-charged weigh-in! Reggie Theil and Larry Mote both finished 9th and 11th, respectively. So those big fish were out there where I was fishing. I just didn't get them in the boat. I think I would have needed the spot all to myself, and actually thought that would happen. But I've got to hand it to those guys. They stuck it out and were there when the fish came up to bite. I've got a 1,000-mile drive tomorrow to reflect on the season, but I know this: I gave it all I had. I prefished from dawn to dusk almost every day and I fished every day of every tournament until the last second. I fished fighting a bad cold and flu and I fished in snow, sleet, rain, hail, 40-mile-per-hour winds and 100-degree temperatures. And you know what? In spite of the disappointments, I loved every minute of it!

Sean and Heather will be home when we get there and will be staying with us for a short while until they get a job and place to stay. Probably a couple of weeks. I'll be fishing a tournament with Sean on Lake Winnebago, the same one I fished with Steve last year. That will be fun and I'm already looking forward to it. We'll leave really early and drive straight through, probably getting home about 11 o'clock tomorrow night.

Farm Fleet Tournament
Lake Winnebago, Wisconsin

Saturday, August 15th

It's the first day of the Farm Fleet Tournament on Lake Winnebago and my son Sean and I are feeling pretty good about our chances. I prefished the past three days in all my old spots and located the best and maybe most consistent fish on the edges of the cane beds in Lake Butte des Morts, the first lake upstream from Lake Winnebago. The big lake didn't produce all that well in practise and the fish I did catch out there were small.

These cane bed fish are like bass, hiding on the edge of the thick overhead cover, then coming out to feed at different times during the day. The trick is to be there when they come out. There's a lot of baitfish hanging around the cane beds, so I expect the walleyes to be there. Yesterday I hit one bed and caught a couple of 5-pound fish which would be huge in this tournament. In fact, I would be surprised if 20 pounds wins the tournament.

Saturday evening

We went to the first major cane bed and I was surprised to have it all alone. The river current flows right into this bed, making it a magnet for cruising walleyes. I expected to catch a limit in no time, but by 10 o'clock, we still hadn't boated a legal fish. We stayed too long and it was time to get out of there and move up to the next bed.

We managed to catch three fish out of the second bed and I believe we would have had a limit if we would have gone there first thing in the morning. Sean caught a 3-pounder, which really helped. We were just flipping 1/16-ounce Odd'Ball Jigs and half crawlers on the edges of the cane and in any open pockets we could find. We're actually in the money with our weight of just over five pounds. That's out of 140 boats which tells you how tough this tournament is. I'm counting on our first bed to kick out some fish tomorrow since it didn't today. That's often the way these things work. I know one thing. One hour on that bed tomorrow without a fish and we're heading to the other spot.

Sunday, August 16th

Once again, the first spot didn't kick out any fish. These walleyes simply amaze me sometimes. I caught the winning fish here three days ago and didn't even work the bed very well. I figured it had to be crawling with those big fish. Not so. We blasted down to where we caught our three fish yesterday and decided to really pick it apart. I caught a 2-pounder at around 1:00 and another one at 2:00, just before we had to head in to the weigh-in. Those two fish brought us up into 15th place for the tournament, which is good out of 140 boats. Once again, we were only looking at catching a couple more fish to win, and I know that those fish were there. I don't know what else we could have done to catch them.

As a postscript to this tournament, we went back to the same spot two days later and just goofing around trying to catch some panfish with Sherry and Heather, I caught a 3-pound walleye. Sean just looked at me with a sick look on his face. But that wasn't the end of it. An hour or so later, I whacked a 30-incher that probably went seven or more pounds. Those two fish would have won the tournament for us. Sean's frustration was evident, but he learned a good lesson about some of the things I face from tournament to tournament. Besides, we had fun, cashed a tournament check and enjoyed spending some time together before he begins his new life with Heather.

August 22-23

The Super Pro tournament aired on TNN this weekend, generating a flood of phone calls from people who hadn't heard that I had won. It was almost like winning it all over again and a great tonic for the post-tournament season blues. I'll be speaking at a men's retreat for three days next week at Fort Wilderness in northern Wisconsin and in mid-September going out to the PWT Championship at Bismarck, North Dakota as a VIP and representative of Fisher Boats.

Ted Takasaki, 1998 Professional Walleye Trail Champion.

PWT Championship
Missouri River
Bismarck/Mandan, North Dakota

September 15-19

The PWT Championship was awesome. I only wish I could have been fishing in it instead of watching it. I did have an opportunity to address the huge crowd during the pre-weigh-in ceremony for about 10 minutes, so that was a good promotion for my sponsors. I also signed a lot of autographs and helped a new Fisher dealer from Minot, North Dakota sell some boats. Ted Takasaki won the championship and I was really happy for him. With his win, that made five new PWT winners out of six tournaments this year.

I was thinking about that and realized that in the past 10 years on the Professional Walleye Trail and 49 tournaments fished, there have been 35 winners. There's only been a handful of two-time winners and only three, three-time winners. If you contrast that with the first 10 years of B.A.S.S. where guys won 10 or more tournaments, you can see that professional walleye fishing is a tough sport to consistently win. In fact, there are still several guys who have fished all of the PWT qualifiers and have yet to win, yet are consistent top finishers. That speaks volumes about the skill level of this group, and just how difficult it is to win a major event.

With no one winning more than three tournaments over a 10-year period, it just shows that no angler has come to the forefront to dominate this sport in the 1990's and only two have qualified to fish all nine championships! Several anglers are in a position to change all that, but each year, new, hot sticks sign up and knock off the perennial qualifiers. Some of the younger guys, like Perry Good and Keith Kavajecz have an opportunity to dominate if they stay in it for 10 more years. And there's probably some young guy out there that will start in 1999 and become a dominant force of the 2000's.

I look back at the number of chances I've had to win and the number of tournaments I thought I would win based on prefishing and I should have and could have won at least four or five more, even more than that. But walleyes will humble you in a hurry, and every guy that's fished for the past 10 years can probably claim the same thing; that given the right conditions, weather and bite, they too, could have won four or five.

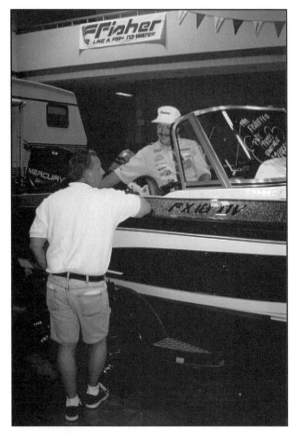

The atmosphere of the PWT championship is awesome. If you can't be fishing in it, going as a representative of Fisher boats is the next best thing.

Reflections on Tournament Fishing

I believe that ethically, fishing is the greatest sport in the world. I believe that just being in the outdoors, enjoying the Lord's creation each day, is a huge privilege, and I think that professional anglers as a whole need to remember that. In the heat of competition, the enjoyment can often get lost. Even guys who have been friends for years can forget, for a moment, that life is much more important than a tournament.

Most of the fishermen on the Professional Walleye Trail have joined the National Professional Anglers Association. One of the goals of the NPAA it to improve the image of professional angling, which in effect means anglers policing anglers. If a member can't meet the ethical standards set forth by the membership, then he is going to be called into account by the organization. If he doesn't clean up his act, the NPAA will not only remove him from the organization, but recommend he not be invited to fish the Professional Walleye Trail.

This might sound harsh, but I believe it's necessary. If the pros don't police their own ranks someone else will do it for them. And that someone else will be people who don't agree with tournament fishing. Now I know that tournament fishing isn't for everyone and that's okay. But I also know that most professional anglers are not only ethical fishermen who release most of the fish they catch whether in a tournament or not, but also have a high regard for the resource, donating time and money to improve fishing access, water quality and the sport of fishing.

Many professional anglers work with kids and we all know that kids are into competition. I know that fishermen can be great role models for kids, especially in contrast to some of the professional athletes that are out there today. Kids need something beyond the internet, beyond TV, beyond video games. They need to learn to not have such an intensive life at such a young age, to enjoy the outdoors and fishing. That's part of what the NPAA is trying to do. We have an association with Big Brothers, Big Sisters and that's a great start. We're also informing corporate America that investing in kids and fishing is a good idea. Kids will buy their products for the rest of their lives. That's something corporations understand.

The future, I believe, looks good. Of course, there are lots of pessimists, but there will always be pessimists. I choose to be an

Walleye fishing is the best it's ever been as evidenced by this 14-pound 4-ounce walleye, caught during the Vanity Cup tournament in Nipawin, Saskatchewan.

optimist. I believe that fishing is better than it's ever been. What it really boils down to is clean water. Period. And that's where the angler has to come in and be a voice. In nature, habitat is everything. I'm also a hunter and birder and I understand the value of ecosystems, habitat and clean water. One small break in the food chain in any system, and it can affect the fishing big time.

All hunters and fishermen should be environmentalists. Not tree-huggers or anything like that, but real activists for clean water in our marshes, rivers, lakes and streams. There is a big move today toward a greater awareness of our environment. It's being taught in our school to our kids. Hunting and fishing isn't part of that curriculum and in fact, is often portrayed as anti-environment. We need to get on the bandwagon, folks, before the whole nation becomes a country of deer-watchers and fish-watchers. Don't laugh. It's already happened in some European countries.

If we can get corporate America to listen and to invest in the future of fishing and clean air and water, we will all benefit. I believe that at the start of the new millennium, we will see professional fishing raised to a whole new level. Out-of-industry dollars will be invested because these corporations have the money and we have the audience. Corporate America has grown weary of paying huge dollars to celebrities and pro athletes that turn out to be immoral or amoral, which gives the company a black eye. The fishing industry is huge, it's wholesome, and it's ripe for the picking. It's just what corporate America needs to not only enhance its image, but to do something positive as well.

Pro angler, Denny Brauer on the Wheaties box is just a start. As corporations have embraced auto racing, so

Corporate America has grown weary of paying huge dollars to celebrities and pro athletes that turn out to be immoral or amoral, which gives the company a black eye. The fishing industry is huge, it's wholesome, and it's ripe for the picking. It's just what corporate America needs to not only enhance its image, but to do something positive as well.

will they embrace professional fishing. It's simply a matter of time, and that time is now. Tournament fishing is here to stay and now is a great time to get involved in it. In tournament competition, you learn a lot, much more than you ever could on your own. Fishing a year on the circuit would be equivalent to picking one of the best fishing guides you know and spending a month with him on 30 different bodies of water. That's how much you would learn. In the PWT's pro-am format, amateurs can learn from the pros under every type of condition and circumstance.

I would encourage anyone who is interested in fishing as a pro, to first get their feet wet fishing the many other walleye circuits out there. You will find out in short order whether tournament fishing is for you. As I said before, I started out fishing in bass tournaments for a $25 entry fee. Today each tournament entry fee on the PWT is $1050.00. That's a big investment and you can pretty much figure that expenses are about the same as the entry fee.

The Masters Walleye Circuit (MWC) started professional walleye fishing, and is one of the premier circuits today. I cut my teeth on that circuit before moving to the PWT with the pro-am format. I made the championship every year I fished the MWC and have qualified for 13 national and world championships since. The MWC really taught me a lot about tournament fishing and I would encourage anyone who is interested in fishing walleye tournaments for the first time, to start there.

As we look toward the future, walleye tournament fishing will only get bigger and bigger. In the year 2000, there will be a tournament that will pay out $250,000 to the winner. That's going to get the attention of out-of-industry sponsors, which means more money will be poured into the profession both on the management end and the angler's end. And if companies can make money or enhance their image by supporting fishermen and tournaments, they'll do it.

Reflections on Life and Family

When I first decided to become a full-time tournament angler back in 1988, it was very tough juggling my career and my family. In fact, in going over one of my old calendars the other day, I noticed that I had my wife written in for six days one year. That's pretty bad, not to mention the time away from the kids. I have to say that there was a lot of selfishness on my part back then. I wanted to be a pro fisherman and if my family had to sacrifice because of it, I was willing to have them sacrifice. I never asked them what they thought. Looking back, I realize how out of balance my life was and how wrong it was to live that way. Yet, my family stood by me as my dream was realized.

1988 was a year of great fulfillment for me, a year of many ego trips. I had won two tournaments; I did a national commercial with Babe Winkelman for Lindy-Little Joe; I had appeared on several local and regional TV shows; I was in several magazines, including In-Fisherman, which was a lifelong dream. I did a ton of fishing seminars, and I made more money than I had ever made before.

Yet, with all this success and the dreams of all those years of being a pro fisherman being realized, I still had an emptiness in my heart and in my spirit that you could have parked a semi in. In September, Mark Dorn invited me to attend a men's retreat with him and I accepted. He said that Al and Ron Lindner would be there, and I thought this would give me a good opportunity to rub shoulders with them and that they could help my career. My motives were totally selfish, but God had other ideas.

You see, in the past, I had always taken full credit for the blessings in my life, and blamed everyone else for my failures. I was a self-made man and I didn't need the hassles of church, God, and always trying to do what's right, in my life. In fact, I had serious doubts that God even existed at all. In my ego and my pride, I had walked about as far as I could from His love, His grace and His protection. But thankfully, He never gave up on me. The second night of the retreat, God revealed himself to me through His Son, Jesus Christ, in a powerful way. I asked Him to forgive me for the way I had been living, told him that I was truly sorry and with His help, I would try to live the life He meant for me to live. With a

A top-10 finish at the 1989 MWC Championship. Back in the late 1980s I thought I was nearing the pinnacle in fishing, but there were some major changes in store for my life.

great wave of mercy and grace, His love and forgiveness overwhelmed me. The cleansing of a lifetime of sin washed over me like a giant, Lake Erie roller crashing over the Port Clinton breakwall.

The change was so dramatic that when I came home two days later and got out of the car, my wife looked at me before I could say a word and said, "you're different!" She was right. In the months ahead, she would see how really different I was. The first thing that the Lord took from me was my cursing, and using his name in vain. How could I ever do that again to the One who died for me and delivered me from my sin? He then gave me a new attitude about my work, my family, and lit a bonfire of love in me for my wife and kids. But that was only the beginning.

I had been drinking pretty heavily over the years, and even more so this year as I celebrated my new-found success as a pro fisherman. But with drinking comes drunkenness, driving drunk, uncontrolled anger, lying, lust, and cursing, not to mention a great waste of money, all sins of my past that I had been forgiven for, but were still in my life. One night, after drinking way too much, I tearfully begged the Lord to take it from me. Again, that great wave of mercy washed over me and I was instantly sober. I have not had a drink since and it's been eight wonderful years.

The depression, discouragement and anger that surface as a result of drinking was gone. I was now able to look at life with clear eyes instead of blurry ones; a clear mind instead of a fuzzy one. The money I saved was used to help others, something that wouldn't have even been a consideration in the past. I began to be concerned about my friends, I became a better listener. I wanted to share with them the peace that God has given me, that He is real, that he loves us so much that he sent his Son to die for us, because He knew that as humans, we could never be good enough.

When Jesus said "I am the Way, the Truth and the Life; no man comes to the Father but by Me," I realized that I, and everyone else, needed a Saviour; that only through Christ would I ever get to the Father and spend eternity in heaven. I realized, too, that it was more than just believing it in my head, but I needed to believe it in my spirit and in my heart. When I asked Christ to come into my heart and into my life, because He will only do that if asked, He responded to my request. God doesn't force anyone to accept His free gift of salvation. But if we only ask, He will give it to us.

My faith is more important to me today than tournament fishing or anything else. God promises that if we seek Him first, He will give us all the other things we need. Most of all, he gives us peace. You lay your head on the pillow at night, and you have peace. You wake up in the morning, you have peace. I know in the tournament fishing game, there are a lot of guys who have no peace. They keep striving for goals and are left disappointed and empty. Been there, done that. But God cares and Christ can turn a person's whole miserable life and attitude around in seconds. He did it for me and has for millions of others.

Could I have been a successful tournament angler without God? Of course. There are many things that we as intelligent human beings can accomplish without God. But you see, that's the problem. Self-gratification and the praises of others only lasts as long as there's someone to see it. Then when you're all alone, the emptiness returns. But when God is glorified, that glory remains, and He in turn honors us for giving Him the glory for our success.

I know that God has given me the talents to fish, to speak, to write and to communicate to others and that He desires that I use those talents for Him, not for myself. The lines of right and wrong have been blurred in this decade and millions of people have been living their lives in a spiritual vacuum as a result. They need to hear the truth and they need to know the Truth!

There's a passion in my heart to reach out to my fellow fishermen and hunters, many who have never heard about the saving grace of God and the eternal life He has promised. I want them to see that you can be a committed Christian, serve God, and still be successful in the eyes of the world. See, what people don't understand is that when we try to do everything on our own, using our own talent, our own wisdom and we fail, we become so discouraged and disheartened that we are no good to anyone else.

That's how I was in the past, but now I know that if I do my best and still fail, I can be an encouragement to others. You see, in the eyes of the world, you failed. But in God's eyes, because you did your best for Him, you succeeded. So I know that I'm successful in His sight, and isn't that a little bit more important than being successful in the eyes of the world? Now when I see another pro experiencing great discouragement, I can be an encouragement to him because I've experienced what he's going through.

When he asks "How come you handle this so well?" I can tell him, "Well, this isn't the most important thing in my life." Then I can share with him what is, and that's the promise of eternal life through Jesus Christ and that's great hope. This other stuff is just temporary, but having eternal hope really does change your outlook on how you fish, how you work, how you live, how you love and how you deal with other people.

I'm grateful that change came, and I'm grateful that God, in spite of how I was living my life, still loved me and still provided a way, not only to heaven, but out of a life of not doing what's right. And God showed me in a real way this year, that serving Him is worth it all.

I came into 1998 pretty discouraged about last season. Now I know that God is not the author of discouragement and I knew all the right verses to stand on and I really began to seek the Lord to remove the discouragement and to give me direction for the future. I just wasn't having much fun fishing tournaments, and I couldn't put my finger on what had changed.

During an intense time of praying, the Lord revealed to me that

The year 1997 was one of the most frustrating in my career and I lost my focus at times. Good friends like Al Lindner help me keep it all in perspective.

I had pushed him aside last year, that the tournaments became more important than Him. He was right. Prior to last season I would spend an hour or more each morning reading my Bible and praying for the tournament, my family, people who were struggling, people who were sick and so on. But when the season started, I would get up and just hook up the boat and get ready for the day without praying. I had indeed, been pushing God aside and I said, "Lord, no matter what happens this year, You're going to be number one and winning a tournament is no longer going to be a priority over you."

God honored that commitment by giving me the Super Pro win. You see, that's exactly how He works. When we finally come to a point in our lives when He becomes the most important thing, then and only then, will He give us, as promised, "the desires of our heart." It doesn't mean we have to become a monk or some great religious leader. That's not what this is all about. It's just acknowledging that He is Lord, that He orders our steps and understanding that if we call ourselves "Christians", (ie; followers of Christ) we will not be blessed if we don't bless God. If we don't honor Him, how can He in turn, honor us? I knew for certain that because I made the choice to honor Him and bless Him, He returned the blessing in the form of the tournament win. By doing so, He once again proved his faithfulness to His word, and I give Him all the glory.

One of the saddest things I see today is the selfishness and greed that is so rampant in this country. Everything has to be put aside so that a person can be successful. I lived that same lie for a lot of years and if there's one regret I have in this life, it's that I didn't spend enough time with my kids as they were growing up. I was simply to consumed with being successful and "doing my own thing" and they got pushed aside. I'm grateful for the way my family supported me and still does today, even though I wasn't always there for them when they were younger.

Oh sure, I went to some of their track meets and some of the games, but there was no commitment to it. I went because I wanted to see them, but if something more important to me was going on, then I did what I wanted to do and that wasn't right. I see people today sacrificing their kids on the altar of success and then they wonder why their kids are turning out the way they are; why they find acceptance in gangs instead of at home; why drugs and alcohol become more important than sports and studying.

If there's one thing I would like to impress upon both Moms and

Dads, but especially Dads, if you like to fish, if you enjoy the outdoors, take your kids with you. You don't have to pressure them into going and don't take them for 14 hours at a time, but if they ask to go, take them. I can remember so many times when my kids, with great excitement in their eyes, would ask: "Dad, can I go?" and I would kill that excitement by saying, "Aw, you don't want to go, I'm going to be gone all day, you'll be bored. You won't have any fun." Even though I could see the excitement fade, replaced by disappointment, I wouldn't give in. Friends, that's tragic. My heart aches right now even remembering those days. How could I have been so selfish?

Moms and dads, spend time with your kids. They grow up so fast and you can never reclaim that time. Here I am, a professional fisherman and I ask my kids who are now adults to go fishing and they can't because they are too busy with their families and jobs. I take my grandchildren sometimes, and that's a blast, but every time I go with them I'm convicted about not taking their mom or dad when they were kids. Parents, take them now and they will never forget it.

Kids are such an important part of fishing. Everyone should be willing to take time to help kids with their fishing.

I leave you with this final story. Years ago when Sean was a kid, we took an overnight canoe trip down the Mecan River near our home. The plan was to canoe all day and catch some fish for supper, then camp overnight and have Sherry pick us up by the next bridge the following morning. Here's how I related this trip recently to Sean's wife, Heather at a family dinner, at least as I remember it.

"It was cold and drizzly the whole trip, and fishing was lousy. Sean caught one 10-inch trout and I caught a snake northern. That would be our supper. We pulled into a sandbar and pitched the tent as the drizzle became a downpour. Not very good at pitching tents, by the time I was done, it looked more like wind had blown it there. The rain continued as I tried to light a fire to cook the trout. After a long time, it finally got hot enough and we ate the semi-raw fish. I gave Sean the trout and I ate the pike, with pungent wet wood smoke blowing in our faces.

"Of course, the smoke helped keep down the millions of mosquitos that were finding their dinner a little bit warmer than ours. We finally retired to the tent, much to the relief of the 100 mosquitos that figured out it was drier, at least for the moment, inside the tent. It didn't take the tent long to start leaking, but Sean didn't notice because he was sound asleep and snoring like a grizzly bear.

"As I lay awake in the dripping tent, I became angry and frustrated with myself for my lack of preparation, my lack of tenting skills, even my inability to at least do what I do best; catch some fish. I had wanted this to be a special time and it was a disaster. By morning, there was two inches of water in the tent, we were wet, cold and miserable. I wondered if Sean would ever camp out again in his life. I knew I wouldn't."

After I told the story, Sean looked at me and said: "Dad, I don't remember any of that stuff. I had a great time. I caught a nice trout and got to go camping and spend time with you and that was really special." I was stunned. Then I realized that even though our time together didn't meet *my* expectations, it far exceeded his. To this day, he loves to camp (I still don't), and he taught me a valuable lesson that kids want to be with their parents when they are growing up and that they remember those times as a blessing. I know I still remember all the things my dad did with me, and I wrote them and framed them in a tribute to him a couple of years ago. We never know how that time together will end up shaping their entire lives.

Thanks, Dad, for taking me fishing.

1997-1998 PWT Top Ten

Dee Zee/Walleye Angler
Walleye Super Pro
Lake Ouachita, Arkansas
April 17-19, 1997

Pro Division

Rank	Name	City	State	#Fish	Wgt	Winnings
1	Chad Hall	Algona	IA	14	38.97	$45,000
2	Ted Takasaki	Algonquin	IL	10	32.40	$15,000
3	Mark Brumbaugh	Pitsburg	OH	12	31.03	$10,000
4	Harry Stiles	Pierre	SD	12	29.39	$8,000
5	Steve Fellegy	Aitkin	MN	13	28.84	$6,000
6	Ross Grothe	Apple Valley	MN	9	23.75	$5,000
7	Perry Good	Eagan	MN	9	22.38	$4,600
8	Mike McClelland	Pierre	SD	10	21.86	$4,400
9	Dan Plautz	Muskego	WI	8	20.36	$4,200
10	Chris Gilman	Mosinee	WI	12	20.01	$4,000
25	Daryl Christensen	Montello	WI	7	14.16	

Walleye Super Pro

Amateur Division

Rank	Name	City	State	#Fish	Wgt	Winnings
1	Charles Tipton, Jr.	Box Elder	SD	10	24.64	$9,000
2	Bill May	St. Louis	MO	8	24.55	$3,300
3	Dan Graves	Renner	SD	10	23.55	$2,000
4	Paul Rump	Maineville	OH	9	22.23	$1,200
5	Dan Stier	Pierre	SD	10	22.12	$1,200
6	Larry Rolince	Vermilion	OH	10	22.06	$1,000
7	David Novak	Milwaukee	WI	8	20.83	$1,000
8	Frank Deja	Stevensville	MI	9	20.67	$800
9	Mark Magura	Valparaiso	IN	6	20.39	$800
10	Dave Stough	Youngstown	OH	7	20.16	$700

Lowrance/Stren Central Pro-Am
Mississippi River, Dubuque, Iowa
May 8-10, 1997

Pro Division

Rank	Name	City	State	#Fish	Wgt	Winnings
1	Chris Gilman	Mosinee	WI	12	25.18	$40,000
2	Mark Martin	Twin Lake	MI	14	23.88	$14,000
3	Jeff Taege	Stevens Point	WI	13	20.18	$9,000
4	Ted Takasaki	Algonquin	IL	12	20.05	$7,000
5	George Freeman	Iron Mountain	MI	10	18.57	$5,000
6	Mark Meravy	Morris	IL	11	18.25	$4,000
7	Keith Kavajecz	Kaukauna	WI	8	17.52	$3,800
8	Mike Gofron	Antioch	IL	10	17.26	$3,600
9	Rick Olson	Mina	SD	11	17.05	$3,400
10	James Klick	Paynesville	MN	10	16.92	$3,200
67	Daryl Christensen	Montello	WI	4	5.57	

Mississippi river, Dubuque, Iowa

Amateur Division

Rank	Name	City	State	#Fish	Wgt	Winnings
1	Steve Haferbecker	Dubuque	IA	11	19.16	$12,500
2	Dave Flury	Dubuque	IA	11	18.68	$4,000
3	Dennis Pickel	Dubuque	IA	11	18.29	$2,500
4	Ronald Brake	Petersburg	IL	10	16.00	$2,100
5	Gary Speicher	Cedar Rapids	IA	6	15.89	$1,800
6	John Phillips	E Peoria	IL	7	14.54	$1,600
7	Mike Rowe	Naperville	IL	4	14.52	$1,400
8	Greg Barry	Springfield	IL	8	14.44	$1,200
9	Steven Safranski	Peru	IL	9	14.24	$1,100
10	Randy Bandstra	Muskegon	MI	9	13.91	$1,000

Champion Midwest Pro-Am
Leech Lake, Walker, Minnesota
June 2-4, 1997

Pro Division

Rank	Name	City	State	#Fish	Wgt	Winnings
1	Dale Dykes	Leon	IA	9	29.85	$40,000
2	Gary Roach	Merrifield	MN	10	27.35	$14,000
3	Chris Gilman	Mosinee	WI	10	24.93	$9,000
4	Paul Meleen	Onamia	MN	9	23.95	$7,000
5	Dan Stier	Pierre	SD	9	23.40	$5,000
6	Perry Good	Eagan	MN	9	22.44	$4,000
7	Roger Gathman	Hartley	IA	9	22.34	$3,700
7	Ron Anlauf	Braham	MN	9	22.34	$3,700
9	John Campbell	West Dundee	IL	9	22.10	$3,400
10	Mark Schultz	Niagara	WI	7	21.79	$3,200
112	Daryl Christensen	Montello	WI	2	2.68	

Leech Lake, Walker, Minnesota

Amateur Division

Rank	Name	City	State	#Fish	Wgt	Winnings
1	Greg McConville	Clive	IA	8	25.56	$12,500
2	David Blow	Fargo	ND	9	25.52	$4,000
3	Jim Miller	Sherburn	MN	7	23.88	$2,500
4	Rick Runquist	Akeley	MN	9	23.68	$2,100
5	Randy Bandstra	Muskegon	MI	8	23.43	$1,800
6	Robert Courage	Pt Colborne	ONT	8	23.30	$1,600
7	Colin Crawford	N Aurora	IL	6	23.20	$1,400
8	James Myszkewicz	Burlington	WI	8	21.28	$1,200
9	Dennis Freidel	Prescott	WI	10	21.37	$1,100
10	Matt Stans	Chaska	MN	8	20.86	$1,000

LubriMatic/PowerBait Eastern Pro-Am
Lake St. Clair - Mt. Clemens, Michigan
June 26-28, 1997

Pro Division

Rank	Name	City	State	#Fish	Wgt	Winnings
1	Dave VanOss	Appleton	WI	18	49.13	$40,000
2	John Gross	Racine	WI	16	40.55	$14,000
3	Gary Gray	Oshkosh	WI	17	40.54	$9,000
4	Tommy Skarlis	Waterloo	IA	18	39.68	$7,000
5	Steve Poll	Fond du Lac	WI	16	39.58	$5,000
6	Ron Seelhoff	Burlington	CO	16	39.31	$4,000
7	Chris Gilman	Mosinee	WI	16	39.23	$3,800
8	Kim Papineau	Escanaba	MI	17	34.52	$3,600
9	Mike Jensen	Maple Grove	MN	16	34.41	$3,400
10	Jeff Taege	Stevens Point	WI	18	33.96	$3,200
36	Daryl Christensen	Montello	WI	8	25.64	

Lake St. Clair - Mt. Clemens, Michigan

Amateur Division

Rank	Name	City	State	#Fish	Wgt	Winnings
1	Dave Sproul	Mt Vernon	OH	17	43.05	$12,500
2	Jeff Gibbs	Trenton	MI	17	40.26	$4,000
3	Steve Bohn	Unionville	MI	18	39.72	$2,500
4	Marvin Yost	Warren	MI	17	39.30	$2,100
5	Larry Bryan	Haslett	MI	16	37.96	$1,800
6	Arlen Wendt	Coon Rapids	MN	18	34.17	$1,600
7	Michael Smolensky	Twin Lakes	WI	16	33.43	$1,400
8	Buck Tihista	Mandan	ND	12	32.97	$1,200
9	John Nuebel	Libertyville	IL	18	32.55	$1,100
10	Dan Wooster	North Branch	MI	14	32.55	$1,000

MinnKota/Pinnacle Western Pro-Am
Ft Peck Reservoir, Glasgow, Montana
July 17-19, 1997

Pro Division

Rank	Name	City	State	#Fish	Wgt	Winnings
1	Perry Good	Eagan	MN	18	56.55	$40,000
2	Leon Houle	Little Canada	MN	11	48.44	$14,000
3	Matt Jacobson	Oshkosh	WI	13	45.59	$9,000
4	Tony Puccio	Madison	WI	15	44.20	$7,000
5	Dave Hanson	Bemidji	MN	18	43.35	$4,500
5	Kent Hutcheson	Pierre	SD	17	43.35	$4,500
7	Todd Grams	Cottage Grove	WI	13	43.07	$3,800
8	Brian Ney	Baudette	MN	18	42.71	$3,600
9	Will Lage	Rapid City	SD	14	41.29	$3,400
10	Marty Glorvigen	Grand Rapids	MN	17	38.99	$3,200
126	Daryl Christensen	Montello	WI	4	5.48	

Ft Peck Reservoir, Glasgow, Montana

Amateur Division

Rank	Name	City	State	#Fish	Wgt	Winnings
1	James Olson	Mead	WA	16	53.57	$12,500
2	Greg Englehart	Marion	IN	14	49.15	$4,000
3	Tim Herink	Plainfield	IL	14	43.47	$2,500
4	Del Zerbe	St Germain	WI	18	41.06	$2,100
5	Charles Tipton, Jr	Box Elder	SD	18	41.03	$1,800
6	Bert Nelson	Billings	MT	18	39.35	$1,600
7	Clay Price	Laramie	WY	15	38.99	$1,400
8	Dennis Freidel	Prescott	WI	14	37.58	$1,200
9	Robert Spannagel	Billings	MT	14	37.38	$1,100
10	David Wylot	Grand Forks	ND	11	37.04	$1,000

Dodge Trucks/Mariner Outboards
1997 Championship
Missouri River, Bismarck, North Dakota
September 11-13, 1997

Rank	Name	City	State	#Fish	Wgt	Winnings
1	Rick LaCourse	Oregon	OH	13	29.79	$50,000
2	Ron Seelhoff	Burlington	CO	14	28.22	$12,000
3	Chris Gilman	Mosinee	WI	14	26.59	$7,000
4	Ted Takasaki	Algonquin	IL	13	25.86	$5,000
5	Mike Theyerl	Two Rivers	WI	13	25.28	$4,200
6	John Kolinski	Menasha	WI	11	24.61	$4.000
7	Will Lage	Rapid City	SD	13	23.66	$3,600
8	James Klick	Paynesville	MN	12	23.23	$3,000
9	Shannon Kehl	Bismarck	ND	12	22.66	$2,600
10	Gary Gray	Oshkosh	WI	12	22.59	$2,100

Dee Zee/Walleye Angler Super Pro
Lake Stockton, Stockton, Missouri
April 17-19, 1998

Pro Division

Rank	Name	City	State	#Fish	Wgt	Winnings
1	**Daryl Christensen**	**Montello**	**WI**	**9**	**22.57**	**$50,000**
2	Norb Wallock	Conover	WI	6	19.54	$17,000
3	Rick Olson	Mina	SD	6	19.21	$12,000
4	Mike McClelland	Pierre	SD	6	16.91	$10,000
5	John Peterson	Bemidji	MN	5	16.43	$7,000
6	Mike Gofron	Antioch	IL	5	16.42	$6,000
7	Greg Horoky	Harrow	ON	6	16.33	$5,400
8	Gary Parsons	Chilton	WI	5	14.44	$5,200
9	Mark Brumbaugh	Pitsburg	OH	5	13.40	$5,100
10	Brian Ney	Baudette	MN	5	12.96	$5,000

Lake Stockton, Stockton, Missouri

Amateur Division

Rank	Name	City	State	#Fish	Wgt	Winnings
1	Rich Crannick	Overland Park	KS	12	28.93	$9,000
2	Chuck Tipton, Jr.	Box Elder	SD	10	28.43	$3,000
3	John Pratt	Roberts	MT	7	23.51	$2,000
4	Roger Combs	Dayton	OH	8	22.54	$1,000
5	Andrew Pukstys	Chicago	IL	7	20.83	$1,000
6	Scott Whitman	St. Clair	MO	5	17.44	$800
7	Greg McConville	Clive	IA	5	14.41	$800
8	Darin Lankford	Chilhowee	MO	5	14.07	$800
9	Bill Meyers	Garfield	AR	5	12.17	$800
10	Leo St. Aubin	Dryden	ON	4	11.45	$700

Stren/MinnKota Eastern Pro-Am
Lake Erie, Port Clinton, Ohio
May 6-8, 1998

Pro Division

Rank	Name	City	State	#Fish	Wgt	Winnings
1	Gary Gray	Oshkosh	WI	15	87.38	$50,000
2	Tommy Skarlis	Waterloo	IA	15	84.39	$15,000
3	Ed Schoenecker	Slinger	WI	15	82.58	$10,000
4	Pete Harsh	Sauk Centre	MN	15	79.79	$7,500
5	Steve Poll	Fond du Lac	WI	14	75.19	$5,200
6	Sam Anderson	Apple Valley	MN	15	74.62	$4,200
7	James Myszkewicz	Burlington	WI	12	72.45	$4,000
8	Ted Takasaki	Algonquin	IL	15	72.32	$3,800
9	Dale Stroschein	Sturgeon Bay	WI	14	70.30	$3,600
10	Pete Parkinson	Ankeny	IA	15	70.26	$3,400
86	Daryl Christensen	Montello	WI	9	42.16	

Lake Erie, Port Clinton, Ohio

Amateur Division

Rank	Name	City	State	#Fish	Wgt	Winnings
1	Charlie Christofferson	Park Rapids	MN	15	89.17	$12,500
2	Royce Drye	Spokane	WA	15	83.29	$4,000
3	Lance Weber	Union Grove	WI	15	83.04	$2,500
4	Jamie Hilton	LaPorte City	IA	15	81.71	$2,100
5	Greg White	Rapid City	SD	15	79.59	$1,800
6	Russell Leppala	Marble	MN	15	75.56	$1,600
7	Dale Frank	Neenah	WI	12	74.76	$1,400
8	Gregory Borgosz	Clarence Ctr	NY	14	74.15	$1,200
9	Steven Haynes	Duluth	MN	15	73.35	$1,100
10	Richard Daniels	Springport	MI	15	72.93	$1,100

Pinnacle/Lowrance Central Pro-Am
Leech Lake, Walker, Minnesota
May 31-June 2, 1998

Pro Division

Rank	Name	City	State	#Fish	Wgt	Winnings
1	Pete Harsh	Sauk Centre	MN	7	22.60	$50,000
2	Dave A. Andersen	Amery	WI	12	19.37	$15,000
3	Ron Seelhoff	Lewellen	NE	10	18.82	$10,000
4	Tom Backer	Fargo	ND	11	18.33	$7,500
5	Mike Gofron	Antioch	IL	12	18.25	$5,200
6	Dave Randash	Dilworth	MN	11	17.32	$4,200
7	Dave Hanson	Bemidji	MN	11	17.24	$4,000
8	John Campbell	West Dundee	IL	11	16.89	$3,800
9	Dan Plautz	Muskego	WI	11	16.05	$3,600
10	Dan Stier	Pierre	SD	7	15.79	$3,400
49	Daryl Christensen	Montello	WI	4	8.96	

Leech Lake, Walker, Minnesota

Amateur Division

Rank	Name	City	State	#Fish	Wgt	Winnings
1	Ray Legatt	Rice	MN	12	21.86	$12,500
2	Lorrie Schaefer	Minot	ND	11	20.59	$4,000
3	David Wallace	Binford	ND	5	16.91	$2,500
4	Bryon Stricker	Brainerd	MN	8	16.55	$2,100
5	John Pratt	Roberts	MT	5	16.41	$1,800
6	Scott Weiskopf	Greenfield	WI	8	16.12	$1,600
7	Tom Miller	Sherburn	MN	7	15.81	$1,400
8	David Blow	Fargo	ND	9	15.45	$1,200
9	Dick Nelson	Warren	MN	8	15.36	$1,100
10	John Hill	Valley City	ND	10	14.86	$1,100

PowerBait/LubriMatic Midwest Pro-Am
Lake Oahe, Pierre, SD
June 24-26, 1998

Pro Division

Rank	Name	City	State	#Fish	Wgt	Winnings
1	Gary Parsons	Chilton	WI	18	69.63	$50,000
2	Chris Gilman	Chisago City	MN	18	60.61	$15,000
3	Dan Stier	Pierre	SD	18	60.39	$10,000
4	Richard Mellon	Pincher Creek	ALB	18	58.41	$7,500
5	Harry Stiles	Pierre	SD	18	58.18	$5,200
6	Dave Spaid	Pierre	SD	18	57.52	$4,200
7	Dan DeJaeghere	Pierre	SD	18	56.80	$4,000
8	Keith Kavajecz	Kaukauna	WI	18	56.40	$3,800
9	Perry Good	Eagan	MN	18	55.89	$3,600
10	Mike Gofron	Antioch	IL	17	54.70	$3,400
74	Daryl Christensen	Montello	WI	18	32.90	

Lake Oahe, Pierre, SD

Amateur Division

Rank	Name	City	State	#Fish	Wgt	Winnings
1	Edward Arbogast	Isanti	MN	18	66.06	$12,500
2	John Phillips	E Peoria	IL	16	58.17	$4,000
3	Andrew Pukstys	Chicago	IL	18	56.17	$2,500
4	Bruce Nelson	Erskine	MN	17	53.77	$2,100
5	Perry Krush	Rapid City	SD	18	53.43	$1,800
6	Greg McConville	Clive	IA	18	53.34	$1,600
7	Cody Hostler	Ft Pierre	SD	18	52.12	$1,400
8	Gary Morris	Blaine	MN	16	51.92	$1,200
9	Christopher Kassube	Stratford	SD	18	50.47	$1,100
10	Charlie Christofferson	Park Rapids	MN	15	49.48	$1,100

Champion Western Pro-Am
Ft Peck Reservoir, Glasgow, MT
July 22-24, 1998

Pro Division

Rank	Name	City	State	#Fish	Wgt	Winnings
1	Scott Fairbaim	Walker	MN	12	56.97	$50,000
2	Tom Backer	Fargo	ND	14	52.84	$15,000
3	Mike Gofron	Antioch	IL	16	46.93	$10,000
4	Norb Wallock	Conover	WI	17	45.67	$7,500
5	Rick LaCourse	Oregon	OH	17	43.65	$5,200
6	Dan DeJaeghere	Pierre	SD	15	42.96	$4,200
7	John Campbell	West Dundee	IL	18	42.40	$4,000
8	Chad Hall	Algona	IA	14	41.28	$3,800
9	Reggie Thiel	Walker	MN	15	40.30	$3,600
10	Perry Good	Eagan	MN	15	39.05	$3,400
81	Daryl Christensen	Montello	WI	9	16.89	

Ft Peck Reservoir, Glasgow, MT

Amateur Division

Rank	Name	City	State	#Fish	Wgt	Winnings
1	Dean Miller	Stevens Pt	WI	14	53.00	$12,500
2	Ken Schoenecker	West Bend	WI	16	51.48	$4,000
3	Lorrie Schaefer	Minot	ND	16	50.48	$2,500
4	Merlin Dressel	Becker	MN	16	48.94	$2,100
5	Dan Glucky	Jamestown	ND	10	42.85	$1,800
6	John Janousek	Hutchinson	MN	15	42.52	$1,600
7	Mike Schamber	Winnipeg	Man	17	41.96	$1,400
8	Kastor Simensen	Nashua	MT	17	41.84	$1,200
9	Mitch Howe	Shepherd	MT	18	40.50	$1,100
10	John Nuebel	Libertyville	IL	10	38.03	$1,100

Dodge/Mariner 1998 Championship
Missouri River, Bismarck, North Dakota
September 17-19, 1998

Rank	Name	City	State	#Fish	Wgt	Winnings
1	Ted Takasaki	Algonquin	IL	14	23.92	$100,000
2	Ron Seelhoff	Lewellen	NE	11	21.14	$30,000
3	Mark Martin	Twin Lake	MI	15	19.78	$7,000
4	Mark Brumbaugh	Pitsburg	OH	15	19.43	$5,000
5	Mike Gofron	Antioch	IL	15	18.97	$4,200
6	Dan Plautz	Muskego	WI	11	18.87	$4,000
7	Pete Parkinson	Ankeny	IA	15	17.84	$3,600
8	Gary Roach	Merrifield	MN	11	16.88	$3,000
9	John Peterson	Bemidji	MN	13	16.86	$2,600
10	John Bergsma	Walker	MI	7	15.38	$2,100